JET ROULETTE

JET ROULETTE

Flying Is a Game of Chance

FRED McCLEMENT

Doubleday Canada Limited
Toronto, Ontario

Doubleday & Company, Inc.
Garden City, New York

1978

904.7
M126j
1978

ISBN: 0-385-11279-3
Library of Congress Catalog Card Number 76–56315

*To my lovely daughter Susanne, who was
taken away in her thirteenth year, and
to the little girl who died in a
Yugoslavian cornfield, I dedicate this
narrative because they were both victims
of someone else's carelessness.*

FOREWORD

Air safety has become a game of chance.

The industry, despite its experience of more than seventy years of flying, cannot cope with the technological advances injected into modern airplanes.

In the decades ahead the air transport industry will move into the supersonic age, ready or not. The already crowded airspace will whine with a new breed of airliner—the supersonics, which at present are undergoing advanced experimentation. The British-French Concorde is the current problem child of the industry.

People have become disenchanted with a transportation system that has polluted their atmosphere with noxious fumes, hazardous chemicals, visible filth and ear-shattering noise. They are confused and apprehensive. And no wonder. Over the past decade more than 12,500 persons have died in scheduled airline disasters. In 1976, a year considered a good year by the industry, 1,332 passengers and more than 100 crew members, as well as scores of non-revenue travelers, died in twenty-six accidents.

The inability to improve air safety was never better exemplified than in the spring of 1977 when within a fortnight some 658 persons died and 200 others escaped death. There is nothing to support the hope that catastrophes will diminish,

particularly when air transport operations are continuing to increase without any control on the reins.

Current airline operations stagger the imagination: there are
22,805,000 aircraft movements at United States airports each
year alone, and some 6.5 million in Canada. Of the 5,551
airliners traveling the air corridors on both sides of the border,
over 3,000 are jets flying at close to the speed of sound. In addition 360,000 private pilots in the United States and 35,000 in
Canada share more than 175,000 smaller planes for business
and pleasure. The only reason the system doesn't collapse is
that all the airplanes are not in the sky at the same time. For
those that are, a total of 18,252 air traffic controllers in the two
countries try to make air travel safe for the 510,000 people who
fly every day.

Those in the air and those who never fly are unaware of the
delicate balance between order and chaos. But the number of
flights, landings, and takeoffs creates extremely complex transportation problems in the sky and on the ground. The safety
gap here and around the world inexorably widens.

If accidents are to be reduced to acceptable limits the problems of the system and the turmoil besetting the industry must
be solved by an enlightened public, whether they fly or are
among the 45 per cent of the population who have never set
foot on a plane.

Jet Roulette is dedicated to this enlightenment.

FASTEN YOUR SEAT BELTS

and

turn

the

page.

CONTENTS

PART I

Air Traffic Chaos

1

Death over Zagreb

In mid-September 1976, two seemingly unrelated events took place that would have a profound effect upon the future of aviation.

At London's Heathrow Airport some one hundred black-garbed mourners filed slowly into a British Trident jet. They were en route to funeral services for their friends and relatives who had died in a horrendous mid-air collision over Yugoslavia on September 10, when 176 persons fell 6 miles straight down into a cornfield. Meanwhile, 3,674 miles away at Washington's Dulles International Airport, all 100 passenger seats in the Concorde supersonic airliner readying for the dash to London were filled for the first time since supersonic operations had begun the previous June.

The mourners on their way to Zagreb were evidence of the failure of a system designed to maintain safety in a jungle of more than 3 million airplanes. By contrast, the capacity load of the Concorde was a sign of acceptance of the controversial supersonic airliner and a portent that in the next decade faster planes would be flying through more crowded skies at speeds two and three times greater than currently.

As the British mourners watched the lush green fields of Buckinghamshire pass beneath their plane, a team of British, German, and Yugoslav investigators were attempting to learn why two airliners with all the sophistication of modern instrumentation, and with the most experienced pilots at the controls, had collided with each other in a radar-controlled airspace.

A mid-air collision is the ultimate failure of the air traffic control system. That it hadn't happened a hundred times before this 1976 tragedy was just a matter of good luck, keen eyesight on the part of flight crews, and concentrated devotion by the air traffic controllers who operate this system.

The Yugoslav disaster was a textbook example of what could happen anywhere at any time.

It was a delightful morning in southern England that September 10. Balmy channel winds swept over the lush countryside of Surrey and Hampshire. Ruth Helm, the twenty-seven-year-old mother of two sons and the benefactor of three foster children, kissed her husband Brian good luck on the doorstep of their cottage in Aldershot, two dozen miles southwest of London, and wished him a good trip to Istanbul on the flight on which he would be co-pilot. It was the last time Ruth Helm would see her husband alive.

At twenty-nine, Brian was a dashing first officer for British Airways. With a carefully trimmed mustache and a manicured beard to complement his angular face and hazel eyes, he was known by the stewardesses on all his flights as "that handsome dog." Waving farewell, he meandered through the hedge-lined lanes from Aldershot to Staines and then veered eastward to intersect the Heathrow Airport entranceway. At seven-thirty he arrived on time at crew headquarters, just a step ahead of his flying mate that day, Captain Dennis Tann, veteran pilot of British Airways, known to his flight attendants and crews as a "delightful man."

Married and the father of three teen-agers, Dennis Tann had been mesmerized by airplanes from the time he was a toddler. Now, at forty-four, a senior member of the airline with which he had spent the last nineteen years, Captain Tann had returned to flying the day before, following compassionate leave because of the critical illness of his father. The Tanns lived

near Windsor in a lovely cottage on Iver Heath in Buckinghamshire. His regular motor runs to Heathrow took about half
an hour, less time than Helm's from Aldershot, but both arrived at the airport within minutes of each other.

Tann, with the RAF mustache trimmed and pointed, was
the epitome of British punctuality, good manners, and relia-
bility. He was a pilot's pilot and looked the part. He was quiet,
efficient, proud of his record and his airline, proud of his wife
and three sons. He deserved better than what was to happen to
him before the end of that morning.

Arriving at British Airways flight crew headquarters for
Flight BE 476 were the remainder of the crew: Acting First
Officer Martin Jonathan Flint, twenty-four; Chief Steward
David Crook, thirty-three; Chief Steward Lawrence O'Keefe,
thirty; Chief Stewardess Anne Pauline Whaley, thirty-two;
Stewardesses Ruth Petersen, twenty-six, of Denmark, Jennifer
Munday, thirty, and Rona Goddard-Crawley, thirty-one, mar-
ried to an airline steward. Both Misses Whaley and Petersen
had been "regulars" on a number of flights by the Royal Fam-
ily.

At nine o'clock the flight for Istanbul was called and fifty-
four passengers boarded the sleek Trident, a three-engine jet
similar to the famous Boeing 727, which is now the most common jet airplane in the world.

After the passengers were seated and the three Rolls-Royce
Spey engines started, the airliner rumbled along the taxiway to
the takeoff pad. Given quick clearance for takeoff, the Trident
roared westward along the runway and sharp at 9:21 A.M., the
three engines, gulping prodigious amounts of air to sustain
their lives, lifted into the air, one minute later than the scheduled takeoff time. The airliner was expected to arrive in Istanbul on time in precisely three hours and twenty-four minutes.
The weather en route was forecast clear with visibility unlim-
ited. The airplane's course would take it over Dover, Brussels,
Munich, Klagenfurt, and Zagreb, at an assigned height of
33,000 feet. Its speed would be close to 600 miles an hour when
it reached cruising level over the Dutch-German border. Zulu

Tango (the air traffic control identification name of the flight) could expect an uneventful trip.

According to rules, the crew checked in at the various air route control centers along the route. The center southwest of Vienna handed over the "on time" flight to controllers at Zagreb in Yugoslavia on an 87-mile-long leg known as Upper Blue Five.

The flight was then cleared on a direct course through to Istanbul by the English-speaking controllers at Zagreb. According to international air industry regulations English is the universal language of the air. All pilots and air traffic controllers must use it. This makes it possible for pilots within a controlled airspace to listen to conversations between controllers and other aircraft and thereby keep informed of other traffic in the vicinity.

There were two other jets in the sky under Zagreb control that morning as the British Trident entered Yugoslav airspace. One was a Lufthansa Boeing 737 at 29,000 feet en route to Belgrade from Frankfurt, and the other was a Yugoslavian Inex-Adria DC-9. Both planes were carrying holidayers between the Adriatic and Germany, a popular route for vacationing Europeans. The DC-9 was a charter run from the holiday resort of Split heading north over the beautiful Dalmatian coast to Cologne, Germany, and carrying 108 passengers plus a crew of 5. It had taken off at 10:48 A.M. and was still climbing to a cruising altitude on a north-northwest course.

At ground level, all three jets were visible as individual bright blips on the display radars of Zagreb's Air Route Traffic Control. A sweeping band of light on each circular screen reinforced the blips before the eyes of the eight controllers who were on duty that day.

One of those controllers cleared the climbing DC-9 to a cruising altitude of 35,000 feet which would take it through the 33,000-foot altitude already assigned to the Trident. International flight rules, when radar is being used, state that aircraft must always be separated by a distance of 2,000 feet vertically and 5 miles horizontally.

Another controller saw on his radar screen the two tiny bars of light approaching each other. Realizing that the rapidly converging blips signaled a possible collision he instantly transmitted a radio warning call to the Yugoslav DC-9 because it was intruding into the skyway assigned to the British jet.

In his excitement he shouted the warning and other directions in Serbo-Croat, his native language. The captain and first officer of the DC-9 could understand him but the crew of the Trident could not; nor could the crew of the Lufthansa.

High-peak excitement accompanied by intense fear can cause a person to revert to his native tongue. This may have happened to the Yugoslav controller. He may have called the Yugoslav pilot in his own language for a quicker reaction to the problem or he may not have wanted to panic the crew of the British plane. Whatever the reason, it was a fatal mistake.

The Trident and the DC-9 were hurtling toward each other at a closing speed of close to 1,200 miles an hour. It is unlikely that Captain Tann in the Trident or Captain Joze Krumpak in the DC-9 had time to see each other. But even if they had received a few seconds' warning, would they have been able to assess the situation and transmit their reactions to the controls? Tests by the Air Lines Pilots Association have shown that it takes approximately eleven seconds to evaluate a problem and to take corrective action.

The pilot of the Lufthansa 737, sliding along at 29,000 feet, was the only witness to the horrifying event of the next second. Captain Joseph Kroese, a Dutchman, had been listening to the conversations between Zagreb Air Traffic Control and other planes in this busy crossroads when he heard an agonized command screamed into the radio system. But the language was Serbo-Croat, as he was later to testify, and he could not understand what was being said.

At that moment, 11:16 A.M., he saw the two planes closing above him, slightly to his right, and he uttered an exclamation of dismay. He saw an explosion, not of fire at first, but of dust and debris, of bits of wreckage like aluminum snow mingled with a quickly forming cloud of compressed air. And bodies. Bodies flying everywhere. Human, spread-eagled, and looking like birds. Then a ball of fire enveloped the DC-9.

Six miles below the collision of the Trident and the DC-9, twenty-one-year-old Luba Panketic was strolling home along a country path between cornfields. She was walking toward the sleepy village of Vrbovec, where a score of small flower gardens that dotted the village welcomed the rising sun. She heard a thunderclap. Later she described it as "a tremendous noise."

She looked skyward, turning to keep the sun at her back and shielding her eyes from the morning glare, and saw little dots falling through the air. Some were directly above her and getting larger.

"The body of a young girl crashed into the ground five yards in front of me," she said. "I screamed in horror. The sky was raining death. Next, suitcases began falling all around me. I began to run and I almost fell over the body of a man."

Within seconds the cornfield was a nightmarish scene beyond belief.

The bloody sight in the field made even hardened policemen weep. One of them, Gavro Tomasevic, cried: "I felt sick. A little girl had survived the crash after plunging 33,000 feet to the ground. She lived for about an hour. She died in the hospital. Poor little thing."

A farm worker rushed to the disaster scene. The first thing he saw was the body of a woman, still strapped in her seat. But her head was crushed and she was unrecognizable. Nearby lay what was left of a man's body after it hit the ground. There was nothing from the waist up. He had been cut in half by the impact in the air.

It was obvious that the collision had torn both planes apart. The Trident lost its right wing and most of the fuselage along the right side. More than half of the passengers in this area were exploded out of the aircraft and fell lazily to the ground to die at impact. The DC-9, after shearing into the underbelly and severing the wing of the Trident, spiraled to the ground leaving a vertical smoke veil in the sky what appeared like a giant tree. One witness described it as looking like Jack's beanstalk.

The Trident plummeted straight down and struck the earth 7 miles from the DC-9. The broken bodies from the English flight would eventually be identified, but those holidayers on the DC-9 charter, many of them honeymooners, would never be identifiable. They were consumed in the prye.

The death toll from the collision was 176—the worst mid-air crash in aviation history.

Back in England, Ruth Helm had just turned on the television to watch "Play School" with her sons when she saw the news flash. She knew instantly that Brian was dead. Mark, three, was too young to realize why his mother was weeping, but Paul, four, knew that his daddy would never come home again.

Mrs. Helm was bitter over the fact that the television and other news media received the news of the disaster before the next of kin of the flight crew.

"When the British Airways people came to see me, I told them I already knew that Brian was dead. But why did he have to die? Why?"

In far-off Yugoslavia, investigators from England and Germany and local authorities were seeking answers to that very question and were prepared to get tough with air traffic controllers involved in air crashes and near-misses in the future. It was therefore no surprise in December 1976 when the Yugoslav board of inquiry blamed its air controllers for the accident. All eight controllers on duty that morning were immediately arrested, charged, and released on bail.

Tapes recovered from the broken airliners and from the Air Traffic Control Center confirmed that communications with all the flights over this busy air corridor were in English. But the final warning of the possible collision was made in Serbo-Croat. If it had been in English the captains of the Trident and the DC-9 might have had just enough time to take effective emergency evasive action.

Moreover, the Lufthansa pilot testified that Yugoslav air controllers regularly used their native tongue and on that ill-fated day he said he heard the Zagreb air controllers talk in their own language when giving the DC-9 a flight path change that put the aircraft into a collision course with the British jet.

Zagreb's deputy public prosecutor, Slobodan Tatarac, told reporters that the alleged controller at the time was Gradimir Tasic, twenty-eight, who was charged with "failure to apply regulations prescribed to keep planes on separate courses." The prosecutor said that Tasic "did not take precise measures to prevent the crash" and alleged that the controller was late in recognizing that a collision situation existed.

The chief of Zagreb Flight Control, Ante Delic, and the chief of Regional Flight Control, Milan Munjas, and five others were also charged with "failure to ensure the use of English in conversations with pilots . . . failure to ensure that subordinates carried out standard regulations . . . negligence in performing their professional duties."

Ten months after the tragedy, a five-member panel of the Zagreb District Court of Justice found Tasic guilty of grave offenses against public safety and sentenced him to seven years in prison for criminal negligence. It was the first time in air history that a controller had been found guilty for an accident. The seven others who were charged at the same time as Tasic were acquitted.

The Zagreb trial increased concern in Canada, where English-speaking flight crews had been complaining that French-Canadian controllers were using French at Quebec airports. The powerful Air Line Pilots Association in the United States immediately cried a warning that its members would not fly into any airport anywhere if English was not the language of the controllers. Thus armed, the Canadian Air Line Pilots Association called a nationwide strike to protect the use of English, but a French-Canadian judge ordered an injunction against the English-speaking pilots. The controversy has not diminished to this day.

Britain's Guild of Air Traffic Control showed concern that the blame for the mid-air tragedy had been attributed solely to the controllers. Len Vass, past-master of the Guild, said the inquiry had paid no attention to the potential shortcomings of the Yugoslavian air traffic control system. But he did not elaborate when he made this charge to *Flight International* magazine in London.

He could have taken a much stronger stand by mentioning

the number of reports made by British pilots concerning recent near-misses over France, Germany, and Spain in particular, or the fact that three mid-air collisions, including the Zagreb disaster, accounted for one sixth of the year's passenger fatalities in 1976. The first involved a Russian Aeroflot and an unidentified jet over Sochi in the U.S.S.R., and the other was between a Cubana DC-8, leased from Air Canada, and a military jet over Havana.

In West German airspace in 1976, alone, 221 near-collisions were reported, a frightening indication of the seriousness of the global situation. British pilots charged that over Spain every flight was fraught with hazards.

Such startling charges of dangerous flying conditions over Europe were much too late to save the fair-haired little girl who lived a few minutes and then expired in the Yugoslavian cornfield.

I wonder what her name was, this innocent victim of a frighteningly outmoded system of transportation.

2

Tragedy at Tenerife

The natives of the lovely volcanic island of Tenerife, the largest of the seven Canary Islands owned by Spain and lying some 70 miles off the northwest coast of Africa, boast that their climate is a perpetual spring where balmy Atlantic breezes mix with tropical sunshine almost every day of the year.

Brooding over the paradise is the 12,192-foot snow-capped peak of Pico de Teide, which translated means the Peak of Hell.

Because of its delightful climate, Tenerife has been a vacation wonderland for Arabs and Europeans since the Middle Ages. Classical writers called the Canaries the Fortunate Islands and expeditions to them were recorded by Pliny as far back as 40 B.C.

But the rains came to Tenerife on March 27, 1977, and with them Hell descended from the mountain peak in a veil of fog to turn the island's airport of Los Rodeos into a holocaust unmatched in the history of aviation.

Incredibly, two 231-foot-long Jumbo 747 jets collided on the airport's single runway. The fiery molten mass of 1,400,000 pounds of fuel and metal consumed and vaporized 575 persons. Four others died later from their burns.

The disaster was an ironic twist of fate. The Spanish Air Ministry in 1972 decided to improve its air traffic control system by modernizing five key centers with modern terminal radar systems coupled to long-range surveillance of Spanish airspace and beyond. Terminal radars were installed at Madrid, Barcelona, Palma de Mallorca, Málaga, and Las Palmas on Grand Canary Island. Tenerife was not included in the modernization plans because Las Palmas was the capital island and by far the busiest. And because it was only some 40 miles from Tenerife, its terminal radar with a range of 50 miles coupled to a beacon radar with a 200-mile range was considered adequate for both islands.

There were, however, two drawbacks at the installation at Las Palmas. The large mountain peak to the west of the airport was an insurmountable barricade to monitoring flights into Tenerife, and the beacon atop that peak, which was supposed to be coupled to the terminal radar, was used by the army and was not always available for surveillance of commercial aircraft operations.

Without terminal radar of its own, the Los Rodeos Airport on Tenerife was isolated from air traffic control. Those on duty in the control tower that day of fog and rain were unable to see any farther than a few hundred feet into the afternoon gloom which cloaked a score of jet airliners that had been diverted to Tenerife because of a bomb explosion in the Las Palmas terminal that morning.

Despite reports to the contrary, Tenerife has a good airport that boasts an 11,155-foot concrete runway, an instrument landing approach system as good as any in America, a control tower, hangars, modern waiting rooms in the terminal, parking ramps and taxi strips that compare favorably with the best in airports serving medium-sized cities. This complex dominates a 2,073-foot-high plateau 9 miles from Santa Cruz, the island's major city.

The only runway was coated in traditional black macadam with border lights and an illuminated center strip. On its north side, separated by a boulevard of grass, was a taxi strip that ran parallel to connect the takeoff holding pads at either end of the runway. Because of the diversion of air traffic that day, Los Rodeos was overwhelmed by jet planes that jammed the tarmac in front of the terminal and clogged the taxi strip to the extremities of the runway.

Shortly after two o'clock, at about the same time as visibility diminished even more, Las Palmas announced to Los Rodeos Airport tower that it was once again open for traffic. The tower at Tenerife immediately announced to all waiting aircraft crews that flights would begin as soon as the traffic was untangled.

A Pan Am Clipper commanded by Captain Victor Grubbs announced that it was ready. At fifty-six, Grubbs had thirty-two years of flying experience; he was assisted by another Pan Am veteran, First Officer R. L. Bragg. The two pilots heard the Tenerife tower confirm they had received the message, but there would be another irritating delay in getting the anxious holidayers to Las Palmas. A KLM plane, under the command of Captain Jacob Veldhuizen Van Zanten, fifty-one, a twenty-five-year career pilot, was being fueled and blocked Pan Am's way. It would require another forty-five minutes to complete fueling.

Van Zanten had decided to fill the fuel tanks of his 747 for the return non-stop trip to Holland rather than do nothing during the long wait at Los Rodeos. It would save him precious time at Las Palmas, several hours at least. But his white- and blue-lettered Jumbo stretched across the parking ramp, preventing any other planes from reaching the runway.

At last, KLM was fueled and ready. It received priority for the takeoff because it was nearest to the runway. Pan Am, having waited all the time, was relegated to second place. The passengers, who had paid between $1,500 and $2,500 for the fourteen-day air and cruise holiday, were already displeased by the time-consuming delays.

Unseen by Captain Van Zanten, the Pan Am Clipper was taxiing behind him in the same runway, but he was aware of it by conversations between the tower and the Clipper. The following exchange took place:

PAN AM: Tenerife, Clipper one seven three six. [Pan Am identifies itself.]
TOWER: Clipper one seven three six, Tenerife.

PAN AM: We are instructed to contact you now and also to taxi down the runway, is that correct?

TOWER: Affirmative. Taxi into the runway and leave the runway third, third to your left. Third. [The tower is telling Pan Am to use the third exit, or taxiway, which is known and marked as Charlie-4. It is the last parallel taxi strip that leads to the takeoff pad. It is slightly more than 1,400 meters from the entranceway of the terminal. Pan Am would have to pass Charlie-2 and Charlie-3, all of them clearly identifiable on the airport map of Tenerife, which all pilots on overseas runs possess in their briefcases.]

PAN AM: Third to the left. Okay.

TOWER: Four eight zero five, how many taxiways did you pass? [The tower is asking KLM this question.]

KLM: I think we just passed Charlie-4 now.

TOWER: At the end of the runway make one eighty and report ready for clearance. [KLM is instructed to turn around and to report to the tower and await takeoff clearance.]

KLM: Okay, sir. Is the centerline lighting available?

TOWER: Stand by. I don't think so, sir. I don't think . . . stand by. I will check. I think they are working on them, anyway I will check it . . . For your information the centerline lighting is out of service.

KLM: KLM four eight zero five is now ready for takeoff and we are waiting for ATC clearance. [Captain Van Zanten informs the tower that he is awaiting clearance from Air Traffic Control with instructions as to the outbound route to Las Palmas.]

TOWER: KLM, you are cleared to the Papa beacon. Climb to and maintain flight level ninety, right turn after takeoff, proceed with heading zero four zero until intercepting the three two five radial from Las Palmas VOR. [Air Traffic Control is advising KLM to make a right-hand turn after taking off on a 300-degree heading. This would put the 747 on a northerly course while climbing to 9,000 feet for the 52-mile hop to Las Palmas. KLM was to maintain this heading until intercepting a Variable Omni-Range radio signal on a 325-degree line from Las Palmas. The aircraft was then to turn south and follow the 325 radial to Las Palmas.]

KLM: Roger, sir. We are cleared to the Papa beacon flight level ninety, right turn out zero four zero until intercepting the three two five. We are now at takeoff. [A tragic misunderstanding (may) have occurred at this point. Was KLM reporting that it was at the takeoff point and starting to go? No takeoff clearance had been given by the tower, which is mandatory procedure. Obviously the tower did not think so. The next transmission was:]

TOWER: Okay. Stand by for takeoff. I will call you.

PAN AM: Clipper one seven three six report runway cleared.

PAN AM: Will report runway cleared. [This means that Pan Am will report when it has fully turned into Charlie-4, which should be at any second.]

TOWER: Thank you.

Seconds after this transmission, the two 747s collided.

At some point during this conversation, which was frequently interrupted by static and perhaps other aircraft voices cutting in, the KLM crew believed that the runway had been cleared by Pan Am and, having received its climbout route and clearance to Las Palmas, that takeoff had been granted.

However, there is a regulation at all airports that the control tower *must* clear a flight for takeoff with the following message: "Flight so and so, you are cleared for takeoff."

The answer from the plane must be: "Flight so and so, cleared for takeoff. Roger."

The next message from the flight should be: "Flight so and so, rolling."

The tower will then reply that it is clearly understood the flight is rolling down the runway.

No such transmission took place. Both Dutch and Spanish officials said the KLM plane started the takeoff without final clearances, but William R. Halen, the chief of the team sent by the National Transportation Safety Board, would not comment on that conclusion.

Asked if there were any deletions in the tower tape recording, a spokesman for the NTSB said: "I have not heard anything like that . . . not even a rumor or a hint."

The fatal rendezvous was impossible to avoid. The KLM was hurtling down the runway, and on reaching takeoff speed of 165 miles an hour the captain lifted the nose of the plane. This is called rotation in jet language. The nosewheels divorced themselves from the runway and the main landing gear was beginning to lift when out of the fog the Clipper appeared in Van Zanten's windshield. There was no way to avoid the collision.

Captain Grubbs said he shouted, "What's he doing? He'll kill us all." But this transmission was not recorded in the cockpit recorder of the Clipper. What the Dutch crew said has never been reported.

In a split second the entire top of the Pan Am fuselage was opened like a tin can. Both wings collapsed on the runway, the engines still running. Captain Grubbs reached up to pull the fire control handles but he reached into open sky. The Pan Am crew fell into the first-class compartment below as the airliner disintegrated in a series of violent explosions. Flash fires and further explosions enveloped the Clipper in dense clouds of smoke.

The Flying Dutchman, with its relatively youthful KLM passengers, including three infants and 48 children under eighteen years of age, slammed into the runway in a tangle of broken fuselage, careening engines, and tons of vaporized fuel. The explosion was like an atomic bomb. All 234 passengers and 14 crew members died in the inferno that followed. Identification of the pieces of charcoal that once were living humans would be impossible. Of the 331 persons aboard the Clipper only 67 survived, and 4 of these would die later of burns.

Pan Am's co-pilot Robert Bragg, after watching in shock as the lights of the Dutch Jumbo hurtled toward him, feeling the shock of the collision and the wall of fire to his right, grabbed a dangling cable, slid down 5 feet of it, and then jumped to the ground 25 feet below.

"When my colleagues in the cockpit tried to get out they jumped or fell into the first-class section, which was burning," he recalled. Although he broke his right foot in the jump, Bragg hobbled back through smoke to an area where several dazed passengers were standing, staring transfixed at the wall of fire that had seconds before been their proud jet.

"It's amazing how people will just stand around at a time like that," he said. "My concern was to get survivors out of the plane, but I had to stop two girls who were trying to get back to reach their mother. She died. They would have gone too if they had reached the broken fuselage."

Pan Am stewardess Dorothy Kelly, thirty-six, of Fitzwilliam, New Hampshire, confirmed that surviving crew members did their best to get to trapped victims, who could be seen through the flames. She was credited with saving the life of Captain Grubbs. She saw him in a mass of burning grass and, grabbing him by the feet, dragged him clear. But such deeds of heroism were rare. Most survivors were injured and many of them badly burned.

Jim Naik, thirty-seven, who had been seated in the first-class section, was fortunate to be blown out of the plane on the first explosion, but his main concern was to go back and search for his thirty-four-year-old wife, Elsie. Naik, a comptroller for the Royal Cruise Line which chartered the Clipper, had only a few scratches on his hands and face. As he started back he was met by vicious billowing heat. He managed to get to the side of the plane and tried to pull his unconscious wife from the seat in which she was trapped. She had been struck on the head when the fuselage sagged.

"I was struggling to get her free," he said. "We got separated. It was like a movie. The plane went up completely in flames. People were tumbling down out of the lounge on top of me and now as I was still trying to get back to the section, a body fell beside me. It was my wife. Oh God, I couldn't believe it. She was alive. I knew she would pull through." She did.

James Novik, a shipping lines official from San Francisco, was also seated in the first-class section when he heard an explosion. Then the ceiling caved in. A piece of ceiling fell on his wife as he was attempting to unfasten her seat belt. There was another explosion, this time more violent. It blew his wife out of the plane and he jumped out just before it was engulfed in flames. He dragged her to safety.

But others were not so lucky. Bodies burned beyond recognition were scattered in the tall grass alongside the runway, which was burning brightly from the cascades of flaming fuel that fell like rain. By the time the airport fire department arrived at the scene in the fog, all hope of rescuing other trapped passengers was impossible.

Doctors and nurses rushed from nearby city hospitals and from as far away as Las Palmas to tend the injured and dying and assist in locating bodies when the ashes had cooled, almost twenty-four hours later. Some of the medical team had already experienced such a disaster. At the same airport on December 3, 1972, a chartered Spanish airliner carrying tourists home to Germany exploded and burst into flames, killing all 155 persons aboard.

It took two days to get the badly burned survivors to the Brooke Army Medical Center in San Antonio, Texas, but only twelve completed the journey. Two died en route and two others would expire later.

Both airlines claimed their dead, all unidentified, and flew them home in crude wooden coffins.

Other than the almost impossible job of identifying the dead, the next duty of the authorities was to determine what had caused the accident, the worst ground collision in history. The question uppermost in the minds of investigators from Spain, Holland, and the United States and in the minds of people all over the world was why Captain Van Zanten, a man so experienced that he spent half his time training other KLM pilots, had rolled into his takeoff without informing the control tower of his intentions.

Had he not heard the Clipper reporting that it had not cleared the runway? Was there radio interference sufficiently strong to garble messages between other planes and the tower? The tower had admitted electrical problems involving the centerline lights of the runway. Could these problems have affected radio transmission?

But electrical problems or not, collisions are mostly caused by human error. How many persons were actually involved in the possible chain reaction of errors may take as long as two years to ascertain. But right from the moment that the crash was reported to the Spanish Air Ministry, the government quickly announced that no blame could be attached to their controllers. Only the investigation of the cockpit tape recorders of both 747s and the flight data recorders of both could supply the evidence of guilt.

The Dutch government acknowledged that the KLM was not cleared by the Tenerife tower for takeoff. Pan Am denied the Dutch suggestion that its Clipper had missed Charlie-4 taxiway. So the battle lines were drawn between Pan Am, KLM, and the Spanish government as to who was responsible for the 579 deaths and the scores who were injured, some of whom will be crippled and scarred for life.

The courts over the next decade could decide the divisions of liability. Jumbos are high-risk business and insurance must be spread among many companies in many nations. Lloyds of London, which spread the risk, announced that it had paid a total of $63 million for the loss of the two jets, $177 million to the familes of the dead as the international liability of both airlines, and $40 million in the travel insurance policies carried by the victims, mostly Americans.

Both Pan Am and KLM are signatories to international agreements limiting their liability to $58,000 a passenger. But American passengers are subject to U.S. law, which removes the limit of liability if negligence can be proven.

The sons of two California women killed in the crash filed a class action suit in the U. S. District Court in San Francisco on March 31, 1977, for each of the 306 Californians who were victims of the Clipper, for a total of $1,989,000,000. Defendants named in the suit were Pan Am, KLM, and the Boeing Corporation, who built the 747. Lawsuits to be filed in Holland would skyrocket the claims to a possible $3 billion, and if all were successful, enough to bankrupt all of those involved.

Can the industry survive such costly disasters?

3

Air Traffic—Control or Chaos?

Air Traffic Control is designed to shepherd airplanes along the skyways, in and out of airports, and to prevent them from colliding in the air and on the ground.

Why does this system have recurring failures?

The answer is simple arithmetic. There are too many planes flying in a limited airspace, some under control, some not under control. There are big planes, little planes, fast jets, and slow planes—and they all concentrate around large cities and along the invisible airways that connect them.

The weak link in the system is the human at the controls, both at the air traffic centers and in the aircraft themselves. There is probably not a commercial pilot flying today who has not experienced at least one near-collision in a flow of continuous traffic where a simple mistake on the ground or in the air is a one-way ticket to disaster.

While the Spanish Air Ministry was investigating the details of the Tenerife crash and the problems in their Air Traffic Control system, two frightening incidents occurred to one airliner within minutes—both of them in Spanish airspace.

On April 14, 1977, Captain Derek Baker of British Airways was flying his Trident from London to Valencia with eighty-two passengers aboard. At 0926 hours he reported: "We and the Jumbo (747) were approaching each other at 450 mph when I banked." At 0936 hours, the same captain reported: "Air Control instructions would have taken us into the path of a Boeing 727."

On the first occasion, he was reaching down to put his landing instruction book down when he chanced to see an El Al 747 at the same height, 33,000 feet. He had to pull his airliner upward to avoid the Jumbo flying across his path.

"There were two or three seconds to make the decision to climb up and over the Jumbo. We were at right angles to each other and 800 yards apart when I banked and climbed up. Conditions were clear at the time or I would not have seen him. I was later told he was on a flight from Tel Aviv to Madrid."

Baker and his co-pilot were unable to call the El Al aircraft because their radios used different frequencies. Captain Baker then tried to rouse Air Traffic Control but received no answer. He reported this to the British Aviation Authority. It was at this point that the other plane entered the drama.

Ten minues later he was instructed by the Barcelona ATC to descend through the path of a Dan-Air Boeing 727. The Dan-Air had taken off from London's Gatwick Airport before the Trident flight, but at the higher speed the Trident overtook the 727. Baker was at 21,000. Baker was told to descend 8,000 feet, but this would have taken him into the path of the Dan-Air. Because both planes were flying the same course and had been in contact with each other, they were able to take evasive action.

Captain Baker charged that Air Traffic Control in Spain is not equipped with en route radar, despite the fact that Spain announced that such equipment had been installed in 1972. Curler-Hammer and Texas Instruments in the United States confirmed that they had indeed installed the system at that time.

Four previous near-misses over Spain were reported to the International Federation of Air Line Pilots Associations in London during the eighteen months prior to Baker's near-miss.

The day after the Spanish incidents, a Jumbo jet crash was narrowly averted at Johannesburg's Jan Smuts Airport and the circumstances were similar to those at Tenerife, according to the *Rand Daily Mail*. The pilot of a South African Airways airbus on a flight from Capetown was 300 yards above the runway and about to land when the pilot noticed a Boeing 747 taxiing for takeoff on the same runway. He pulled up sharply and later simply described the incident as "rather dangerous."

In the United States, a series of four spine-chilling near-encounters occurred during a fifteen-day period in 1975 and thoroughly alarmed the industry—but obviously not enough. The first was on the evening of November 26, when two Jumbos almost collided southwest of Detroit in one of the most intensively controlled air corridors in the world. Just twenty minutes after American Airlines Flight 182 zoomed off O'Hare with 150 passengers bound for Newark, a TWA Lockheed 1011 suddenly appeared. It was identified as an airliner by its pulsing strobe lights in the blackness. The American crew dived their jet to avoid a collision. Neither the crew of the TWA nor any of its 163 passengers were aware of how close they had come to oblivion, but 24 persons aboard the American flight were injured. The investigation into this near-miss was into its ninth day when another hair-raising incident occurred 60 miles northeast of Chicago.

About five o'clock on December 5, TWA's Flight 403 from Hartford with 70 passengers aboard started its descent toward O'Hare, lost in the last rays of the winter sun. Suddenly out of the gloom the pilots saw another jet ahead and just a little below them, but definitely on their descent path. The other airliner was United's Flight 291 operating from Providence to Chicago and inbound to O'Hare on the same heading but slightly below the TWA and on a shallower descent.

With little time to think, the captain of the TWA swung the wheel to his left. The collision was narrowly averted and again the crew of the other plane and its 53 passengers were unaware of how close they had come to disaster. The Safety Board believed the incident could have been caused by a misreading of instruments.

At almost the same time that this was happening, a North Central Airlines Convair 580, Flight 112 from Janesville, Wisconsin, to O'Hare and a private Cessna 421 (a twin-engine craft) en route to Palwaukee Airport, in suburban Wheeling, nearly ran into each other 40 miles northwest of O'Hare. Both pilots took evasive action and reported the near-miss to the FAA.

Ironically, Chicago's airport, the busiest in the world, did not have the electronic warning device that alerts controllers that aircraft are within two and a half miles of each other. It was not installed until 1976, although such area conflict alert systems were in operation at Fort Worth, Denver, Memphis, and Kansas City for some considerable time before this.

Then, on December 11, 1975, at 11:37 A.M., an alert controller at the Washington Air Route Traffic Control, located at Leesburg, Virginia, saw two blips approaching each other. One blip was Eastern Airlines' non-stop from Washington's National Airport to Tampa, the other was an Air Force F101 fighter. Instruments in each aircraft revealed their height to the controller's radar screens; they were both at 19,000 feet.

"Eastern one eight five—turn . . . make a three sixty turn to the left as fast as you can, please," urged the controller, attempting to sound calm so as not to alarm the flight crew.

"Ah . . . three sixty left," answered Eastern without asking for an explanation at that moment.

The controller continued to watch intently as the Eastern plane started its lazy turn to the left, but the fighter, still closing at a high rate of speed at Eastern's one o'clock position, was now a scant 5 miles away.

"Tighten up that turn," the controller ordered with more urgency in his voice.

Thirteen seconds later the controller advised Eastern to climb to 35,000 feet "and no delay, please."

Seconds after this message, Eastern's captain calmly called: "Ah, this is one eight five . . . We dived to miss him . . . Ah, can we go back on course now?"

In the following year, 1976, in the United States, which boasts the most sophisticated air traffic control system in the world, there were 207 near-collisions, in addition to countless incidents that were never reported. Sixty-one of those under investigation involved commercial airliners.

A report of the situation by the Air Line Pilots Association said: "The problem is much more serious than reports of near-collisions would have you believe." In support of this, pilots have reported as many as thirty near-misses in a single month in the airspace involving New York, Washington, and Boston. How many were unreported will never be known.

In Europe, reports of near-misses occur every week. There is no automated conflict alert system that can warn a pilot of a converging aircraft. In the United States, however, the alert system is in operation for all aircraft flying above 12,500 feet. The system alerts the Air Route Traffic Control and tower controllers when the computer perceives a possible conflict between two aircraft based on their position and altitude as reported by automatic altitude-reporting transponders.

Transponders are relatively new to Air Traffic Control and currently are part of the standard radar equipment aboard commercial jets in the United States, but are lacking on most aircraft operating elsewhere in the world because there is no ground-receiving equipment to accept the flight data.

Transponders are simple sensing systems that flash the identification of the operator, the flight number, the air speed in knots, and the altitude of the aircraft to Air Traffic Control. This information is contained in a small rectangular space, hardly more than a quarter of an inch, next to the identifying blip of the aircraft. The blip itself is a tiny line on the radar screen that is reinforced once every minute by a sweeping beam of light.

For instance, American Airlines Flight 1 from New York to Los Angeles flying westbound at 38,000 feet at 270 knots would appear on Air Traffic Control screens all across the country as

AA 1

38 270.

This information enables the controller to know precisely the position, speed, and altitude of every transponder-equipped aircraft on his screen, covering hundreds of miles of sky. The heading of the aircraft is indicated by the changing position on the screen, which is calibrated in degrees of the compass. For non-transponder-equipped aircraft, the controller can see the blip but must request altitude and speed from the pilot of the aircraft.

In this manner, he is able to keep flights at 2,000 feet of separation and 5 miles apart above 29,000 feet in an airspace known as the jet corridor. Where radar scanning is not available, aircraft must be programmed to fly between 10 and 20 miles apart with 2,000 feet of altitude between their pathways. Near terminals, controllers can guide aircraft with 1,000 feet of separation between planes and 3 miles horizontal distance.

Because every flight over 12,500 feet is under control with transponder assistance, flights under that altitude present a constant danger. The greatest potential for a mid-air collision is in this space where smaller airplanes are flying around big passenger jets when they are climbing upward or descending toward the terminals. Aviation agencies and pilots agree that before the end of this decade a system must be devised for collision-alert systems under 12,500 feet. The cost of such sophisticated airborne equipment for small aircraft makes the scheme impractical and impossible unless the government is willing to underwrite such radar protection systems. And this is unlikely.

Meanwhile, the problem of keeping the skyways as safe as humanly possible is left to the controllers with the mix of all aircraft, electronically identified or not.

Most people associate controllers with the glass-enclosed towers that are familiar at every airport and manned by a half-dozen or so men and women watching radar screens or looking out the windows and talking to the pilots of approaching and departing aircraft as well as handling ground movements at the terminals.

Yet the more than 16,000 controllers in the United States and the 2,250 in Canada are not in glass towers, they work in the semi-darkness of windowless labyrinths that are called Air Traffic Control centers. These centers may be located at airports or far out in the country—but it really doesn't matter where they are, as long as every section of the airspace is covered by their surveillance.

Before each controller is a large radar screen showing the designated area for which he is responsible. It may be Departure Control, Arrival Control, En Route Short Flight Traffic Control, or High Altitude Transcontinental Air Traffic Control.

As each aircraft begins to leave the screen of each designated area, it is "handed off" to the next center along the line of flight by a voice signal from the controller, who tells the flight crew to change frequencies and call the next center. At the same time, or sometimes earlier, ground electronic equipment has already notified each center along the route when to expect the appearance of each flight.

But fast water never runs smooth. Controllers must adapt to ever-changing circumstances that affect flight patterns. Thunderstorms can change routes. Clear air turbulence can force a crew to ask for another altitude and heading. Malfunctions of equipment on the ground or in the air can cause delays that multiply dramatically at peak hours. Fog at terminal areas, windstorms, and freezing rain or ice can create appalling conditions for landings and takeoffs, and hundreds of planes have to be stacked up in holding areas far away from their destinations —stacked as far away, in fact, as the length of the continent. Changes in active runways due to wandering wind direction, and also mandatory changes because of pollution and noise abatement procedures, can switch the traffic patterns of hundreds of aircraft within minutes of landing or taking off. These constant changes increase the element of danger and create extra work and an additional strain for the controllers.

The problem of noise abatement affects airport operations. Captain Harry Orlady, a twenty-five-year veteran with United Airlines, says: "Noise abatement procedures force you to fly as close to danger as you dare to. You don't have much margin for error." The air traffic controllers have no control over this situation.

The FAA in the United States and the Ministry of Transport in Canada make these laws, but jurisdiction and enforcement differ in each country. Airports in the United States are operated by municipalities. In Canada they are run by the Ministry of Transport.

For instance, the Port of New York Authority operates three airports within the Greater New York area—Newark, La Guardia, and Kennedy—and is responsible for noise and pollution within the boundaries of those airports. Immediately after takeoff, when the big jets are struggling to get airspeed and require maximum power in all engines, the FAA has the power to force the climbing jets to decrease power immediately after they have crossed the airport perimeter. This is usually after specified hours at night, mostly after nine o'clock. Reduction in power is mandatory in all circumstances unless there is a threat to safety.

As an example of the Canadian regulations, the active runway at Toronto International Airport is changed every two hours after nightfall. One group of residents a mile south of this airport makes it a dedicated chore to watch runway changes during the evening hours, and if there are delays in the change-over the jangle of phones at the airport transport office demands action.

On receipt of such complaints, the supervisor of the Air Traffic Control Center will order the departure and arrival controllers to "change runways" and this takes effect immediately unless there is a condition on the new runway that could cause a safety hazard.

Controllers refer to this constant complaining from residents as "pure harassment." A captain of an airliner will have his jet slowed down and be approaching Toronto's north-south runway when he receives an order from the arrival controller that he must turn and make another approach to another runway.

"Why?" asks the captain if he is not familiar with Canada's laws.

"Sorry, sir," replies the controller, "but noise abatement forces us to change runways."

On the change-over, all planes in the air and on approach must swing to a new heading, speed up engines, consume more fuel, and irritate the flight crews, often tired after long flights. Planes on the ground waiting for takeoff clearance will then be commanded to travel to another runway and line up again for takeoff.

The noise and air problem that faces controllers and endangers flight crews was created many years ago when subdivisions of homes and apartments were permitted by municipal zoning boards to move closer and closer to airports. In desperation, municipalities and government agencies looked around for other sites in the seventies. When suitable acreage was found there would be an immediate outcry from property owners for miles around, and politicians, afraid of the gathering storm, managed to have such plans shelved.

An airport-saturation survey conducted several years ago for the U. S. Department of Transportation had this to report: "The safe solution for the noise abatement problem is land use, including extended runways, planting of rows of pine trees to absorb noise, adopting zoning laws, greater concern to future airport site selection—and, of course, sacrificing passenger 'convenience' to both passenger safety and the hearing comfort of populated areas through utilization of existing airport facilities farther from urban centers."

Everywhere the issue was being fought to a standstill. Leadership from government agencies charged with the responsibility of operating airports was totally lacking. The industry, well-known through all the years for its poor public relations, stayed clear of the gathering storm. Yet its own surveys show that a startling growth of aviation is expected over the next decade, with a greater use of smaller aircraft for business and recreational travel and a whopping increase in Jumbo jets for the commercial segment of the industry.

General aviation has a current fleet of approximately 175,000 aircraft. This will expand to 267,000 aircraft by 1988, one survey revealed. Such expansion will increase air traffic control operations by 72 per cent, with 21 per cent coming from the commercial fleet and 79 per cent from general aviation. Because of the increased use of Jumbos, airline activity is expected to drop 2 per cent, but current orders with Lockheed, who build the 1011, and Douglas, who build the DC-10, and Boeing, who build the 747, show a steady increase.

If the air traffic controllers are under pressure now, what will the situation be for them in ten years' time? Is the answer to build more airports to relieve the burden on those now in existence? Right now, no one will hazard a guess. "Airport" is the dirtiest word in the dictionary and the mere mention of it inflames thousands of people who refuse to face the realities of the future.

4

The Growing Pains of the 747

Tenerife was not the first time 747s got in trouble. Although they are a marvel of engineering and some three hundred of them are currently in world service, the first flight crashed on its landing at Renton Airport on December 13, 1969. It slammed into an abutment 20 feet short of the runway with the top test pilots and engineers flying and monitoring the approach. It slid an incredible 3,500 feet and fire erupted in two of its four engines. Because it was a first flight, fire engines were standing by and quickly extinguished the flames.

It was not until August 26, 1970, that the Safety Board released its findings in the case: "The premature touchdown of the aircraft during a visual approach to a relatively short runway, induced by the pilot not establishing a glidepath which would assure runway threshold passage with an adequate safety margin, under somewhat unusual environmental and psychological conditions."

The first fatal accident aboard a 747 was the death of a small child en route to Hawaii. She strangled in her seat belt, which was fastened for a turbulent approach to the islands.

Then, on September 18, 1970, American Airlines Flight 14 to New York City ran into unexpected trouble with its new 747 at San Francisco International Airport. Sixteen seconds after takeoff with the rising sun at its right, the wheels were being tucked away, the altimeter showed 525 feet, and everything appeared to be normal. There was a muffled explosion and a fire warning light appeared on the cockpit panels.

The passengers on the left side, which was away from the sun, could see intense white fire around the engine. Flames were streaming across the wing. The flight crew activated a bottle of fire retardant in the engine, but this did not stop the flames. Another bottle was discharged but the intensity decreased only slightly. An emergency was declared and the aircraft swung lazily toward Runway 28-Left, but that approach had to be aborted because the landing gear and the inboard wing flaps failed to descend. These were activated manually and the flight made another turn toward the airport and landed several minutes later with smoke streaming from the left side. The full load of passengers and crew members escaped down portable steps.

The Safety Board found that the second-stage turbine disk had separated from its whirling hub and this breakup had punctured the fuel lines and caused the fire. As a result of this investigation, changes were introduced into the metallurgy of the turbine blades. Engines already in service which showed fatigue cracking in the blades were immediately removed from service.

But the turbine problems were not new to the 747. The Safety Board recalled that, a few weeks before the American Airlines mishap, an Air France 747 bound from Chicago to Paris, passing over St. Jean, Quebec, experienced an engine explosion. Fire instantly enveloped an inboard engine and the giant airliner began to vibrate. A frightened stewardess offered little reassurance to the passengers when she ran up the aisle to the flight deck screaming, "Fire!" The crew was aware of the problem. The number-three engine fire warning light was flashing ominously.

Captain Jack Mins shut down the engine and activated the fire bottles. He ordered his engineer, René Cobut, to the passenger cabins to assess the problem and handed the controls over to his first officer, Louis Chauveau, while he radioed Montreal Airport declaring an emergency. By this time the fire was out.

Captain Mins then had to make several hasty decisions. He had to land the 747 soon but he could not set the giant on the ground until he had jettisoned the fuel. This posed a serious problem. No captain will jettison fuel if there is a possibility of fire somewhere in the vicinity of the engines, behind which the fuel is sloshing in the wings. He elected to fly all the way to New York in order to burn off the fuel.

While nervous passengers gulped down cocktails and Cordon Rouge champagne, Captain Mins headed south at 18,000 feet while, at New York, fire and rescue equipment was already racing for the runway and all other flights inbound to Kennedy were diverted elsewhere. He kept his 747 moving at 280 knots to burn up as much fuel as possible and he landed uneventfully at New York.

The probable cause of the mishap was determined to be the incorrect assembly of the high-pressure turbine. The Safety Board recommended to the FAA that all assembly records and installations of 747 engines be reviewed and corrected.

The initial problems of the 747 were smoothing out, when on May 13, 1971, a Northwest Orient Airlines plane was climbing out of Honolulu and bound for Tokyo with only thirty-one passengers and eleven crew members when the familiar problem began. At 1,300 feet the fire warning light flashed on the number-three engine position on the control panels. The captain called the tower and declared an emergency. He was on fire.

The 747 began to shake violently. The yoke began to vibrate severely and fuel to the engine was shut down and the fire extinguishers activated. The vibration eased but the fire horn maintained its unnerving screech. The flight was forced to dump 54,000 pounds of fuel before it could land. Cause of the trouble was the familiar turbine disk separation and rupture of the fuel lines.

On July 30, 1971, a Pan American 747 became briefly airborne at San Francisco International Airport and crashed through the approach light system. Flight 845 was a regularly scheduled hop from Los Angeles to Tokyo with a crew change at San Francisco. After becoming airborne, the plane struck the Instrument Landing Approach System at the end of the runway. The flight crew continued the takeoff, however, and flew for one hour and forty-two minutes while assessing the damage, all the while dumping fuel over San Francisco Bay.

During this time two seriously injured passengers struck by flying metal were being given aid by several badly frightened stewardesses. Parts of the airport landing system structure had penetrated the aircraft. Passengers thought the pieces were part of another aircraft and that they had been involved in a mid-air collision. The 747 had, indeed, sustained major structural damage. Luckily, it was maneuvered back to the airport but not without further trouble: twenty-seven passengers were injured while jumping out of the aircraft.

Investigation of this incident revealed an alarming number of irregularities, from the ground up. The pattern started at the flight planning stage when the Pan Am controller determined that the flight would depart on Runway 28-Left because at 10,600 feet it was the longest runway at San Francisco.

However, the controller was unaware that the longest runway had been closed and that the flight had therefore been ordered to Runway 01-Right. But 1,000 feet of this runway had been barricaded to curtail jet blast on the freeway that runs close to the runway at the takeoff point.

The control tower informed the flight that the new runway was 9,500 feet, but the actual length, according to the Safety Board, was only 8,400 feet, which was not long enough for this 747 with the weight it was carrying.

Sheer luck saved this flight from instant disaster when it collided with the light towers beyond the runway. Superb flying experience brought it safely back to the airport. But luck is a rare commodity in aircraft accidents.

Three years later, on the sunny afternoon of November 20, 1974, a Lufthansa 747 failed to become airborne for more than a few seconds and crashed. The disaster occurred at the Nairobi International Airport, in Kenya, East Africa. Nairobi, at 5,800 feet above sea level, boasts a delightful climate and the soft air of high altitudes, a pleasant combination for residents and tourists, but sometimes a problem for aircraft takeoffs. During the flight-test programs of new jets, the pilots fly them to mile-high airports to determine the takeoff behavior at those altitudes.

The flight was bound from Frankfurt, Germany, to Johannesburg, Transvaal, with an intermediate stop at Nairobi. Captain Christian Krock, fifty-four, was at the controls. The flight roared down the 13,500-foot runway, one of the longest in world operations, and began to lift into the thin tropical air, which was 10 per cent less efficient in providing lift.

The Jumbo faltered. The tail began to sink. Passengers felt the sickening drop of the rear end. There was a collision with a 6-foot elevated roadway at the end of the airport. The plane broke in half, slithered into a muddy field, and blew up as jet fuel sprayed through the air like rain.

Thomas Scott, a steward on the flight, began to drag passengers from the broken wreckage in an effort to outrace the spreading fire. The screams of trapped victims were drowned in the requiem of roaring white heat. With two stewardesses, Scott tried to open an emergency door to free some of those trapped. The door wouldn't budge.

Those who failed to escape from the aircraft burned to death in seconds. The funeral pyre of thick black smoke climbed into the sky over Nairobi.

The crash was the worst in the 747's history. Of the 157 persons aboard, 59 died. Two days after this disaster, Lufthansa officials announced the cause of the accident: the front flaps of the 747 wings had not been activated before takeoff.

It was explained that front flaps on the 747 must be activated at speeds under 150 miles an hour in order to provide the required lift for takeoff and during approach. Passengers recognize these flaps because they form a deep curve at the forward edges of the front of the wings. Before takeoff, a lever in the cockpit is used to preset the rear flaps on the trailing edges on the wings at an angle of 10 degrees. The front flaps are activated by the co-pilot through a pneumatic pressure system. If they fail to move into the correct position, warning lights blink on the three panels before the pilot, co-pilot, and engineer.

Officials reported that the front flaps had never been activated. Obviously the pilot had not conducted a pre-flight check-off. What would cause a man of Captain Krock's stature to become careless? Private preoccupation? Age? Or simply the lack of understanding between man and machine?

On the night of December 16, 1975, a Japanese Airlines 747, with 121 persons aboard, tangled with a wild wind at Anchorage Airport in Alaska and was hurled off the runway and into a ravine. There were no casualties.

Despite these incidents, passengers like the massive size of the 747 and have accepted it along with the DC-10 and the Lockheed 1011. Until the next step in the evolution of air traffic becomes acceptable, the Jumbos will dominate the skies while all the older jets will be retired from passenger service and put to pasture as cargo ships, sold off for private use, or destroyed as too expensive to operate.

Because of the problems besetting the introduction of supersonic flight, Jumbos will be the main carriers until at least 1990 and perhaps as long as the end of this century.

PART II

Birth Pains of the DC-10

The McDonnell-Douglas DC-10 was a proud Jumbo jet until its cargo door hatch began to pop. One such incident caused the worst air crash in aviation history. (McDonnell-Douglas)

Firemen begin the grisly task of locating the remains of some 347 passengers who died when a Turkish DC-10 plunged into the ground near Paris. (Associated Press)

French investigators permitted world photographers to take pictures of the bits and pieces that were once a DC-10. (Associated Press)

Unable to identify their loved ones, a Japanese couple offers prayers in front of the largest single piece left of the Turkish airliner. (Associated Press)

Right, only four persons survived the crash of a Pan Am 707 on the lovely island of Pago Pago in the South Pacific. One hundred and one people died.
(Associated Press)

Left, spectators watch the last minutes of a dying Lufthansa 747 that failed to get airborne at Nairobi.
(Associated Press)

Left, a typical thunderstorm cloud of a summer day. The familiar "anvil of the gods" is beginning to form at the upper right corner of the cloud. Under this anvil lurk the dangerous hail showers. (U. S. Department of Commerce, Weather Bureau) *Right, a flier's view from above a churning sea of thunderstorm cells. Pilots are instructed to avoid these lethal cells whenever possible.*

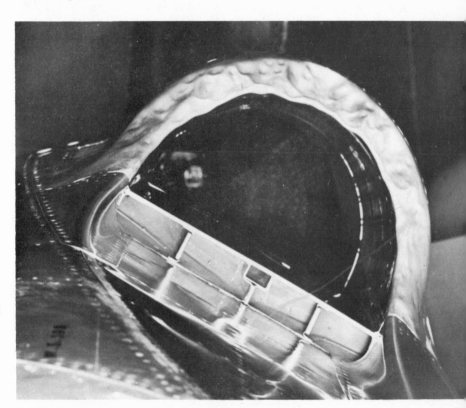

The damage seen on the cowling of this jet engine was caused by hail. (RCAF)

5

The Flying Coffin

It started about twenty-four minutes past nine o'clock on the night of June 12, 1972, when an Ontario building contractor, Sante Facca, raised his eyes from his flower cutting along the border of his driveway to look into the overcast sky. He had heard a strange and unusual sound.

The cloud cover was oyster-gray, reflecting the distant glow of Detroit about a dozen miles to the northeast. He saw nothing. But his keen ears had picked up an intrusion on the stillness of the farm countryside. The frightening whirring noise was getting louder and seemed to be coming straight at him.

Then he heard a dull thud. He remained perfectly still, neither moving across the road toward the sound nor, in mounting apprehension, to the shelter of the front porch.

Now his ears caught another sound unmistakably above him. In a second or two the noise ended with a resounding thump in the soft ground about a hundred feet southwest of where he was standing.

Sante was a curious man and he was not superstitious, nor did he believe in flying saucers or extra-terrestrial visitations. He walked toward the darkening field, where the new corn had reached a height of about twelve inches. Then he saw it. He didn't know what to make of it.

"It" looked like a wooden box bound with steel strappings. It had settled six inches into the soft earth, throwing up a protective moat of soil around the edges. When it occurred to him that the visitor from space looked more like a coffin than anything else he could think of, he dashed for the house and called the Ontario Provincial Police in nearby Windsor.

Other strange things were happening at that moment. Up above the clouds, at exactly 11,750 feet, Captain Bryce McCormick, fifty-two-year-old veteran pilot with American Airlines, was seated in his usual left-hand seat of the Jumbo Douglas DC-10, en route from Detroit to Buffalo and climbing to its assigned altitude of 21,000 feet. There were fifty-six passengers and eight flight attendants in the passenger section.

As his panel clock passed the twenty-eight-second mark after 9:24 P.M. (EST) he heard a loud sound that apparently came from somewhere within the framework of the mighty aircraft.

"What the hell was that, I wonder?" he asked aloud.

A split second later came the sound of the fire warning horn, joined by the altitude warning horn.

"Which one?" queried the co-pilot, First Officer Peter Whitney, thirty-four, wondering which engine was showing a fire warning.

At that instant the door between the cockpit and the passenger cabin flew open. Chief Flight Attendant Cyda Smith was being tossed like a cork along the aisle.

A floor hatch in the aisle next to seat 4-H in the rear section flew up and struck a passenger full in the face. The two stewardesses seated near the dual rear exits were thrown to the floor, which was itself settling into the cargo compartment below. The circular bar in this section was torn loose from its mountings as though an earthquake had occurred, spewing alcohol and glasses along the sloping floorway. Ceiling panels rained down, some of them striking the passengers and making them think the ceiling was caving in.

Five of the stewardesses not trapped by the upheaval at the rear of the plane raced to ensure that oxygen masks had been released and were being used by the passengers. But the release system had been preset to operate at 14,000 feet, and since the aircraft had not reached that height, the masks had not fallen. However, at least one stewardess grabbed a bottle of oxygen from a galley wall and began giving whiffs to the frightened passengers, who were gasping for air in the dust and fog.

On the flight deck, the captain momentarily could not see through the cloud that had formed in the aircraft. He thought he had been involved in a mid-air collision and the windshield had blown out. Dust and dirt blew into his face and the faces of the other crew members as the DC-10 yawed to the right.

"We've lost—lost an engine," gasped Peter Whitney.

"Ah, which one is it?" inquired the captain sharply as his eyes scanned the instrument panel with its many glowing lights. One red glow was brighter and more menacing than the others. It was the fire warning light.

"Two," snapped the engineer. The DC-10 has three engines: number one is mounted on the left wing while number two is located in the tailpiece and number three on the right wing—a configuration that is similar to the engine mountings of the Lockheed Jumbo jet, the 1011.

"Number one is still good," continued the engineer, assessing his panel of instruments and lights, "and . . . ah . . . Captain . . . we'll have to . . . check this out."

The co-pilot cut in: "Okay, we apparently . . . ah . . . the master warning . . . this board's got an engine fire over here, yeah, we got the engines one and three."

This meant that the engines on the wings were operating and were not at present affected by the strange events in the tailpiece.

"Do we have any hydraulics?" asked the co-pilot.

"No," replied Captain McCormick.

Only eleven seconds had elapsed since the fire warning horn had sounded.

A stewardess poked her head through the doorway. "Is everything all right up here?" she asked nervously, her voice high-pitched.

"No," the captain answered as he squeezed the button on his microphone which opened the circuit to the Air Route Traffic Control Center at Cleveland, Ohio.

This center controls all aircraft movements over southwest Ontario from just east of the Detroit River to a point 35 miles west of Buffalo and on a line from 20 miles south of Toronto to 10 miles south of Sarnia. Before takeoff, all flights from Toronto, London, Windsor, Detroit, and Buffalo intending to move into this area must report their intended flights and times of takeoff to the center. These figures are then fed into a computer and the heights and compass headings of all flights are preassigned, so that when American Flight 96 reported to the Cleveland Center soon after takeoff, Cleveland was aware of the intentions of the flight and was ready to monitor its progress across southwestern Ontario and over Lake Erie on its course to Buffalo and New York City.

When American reported an emergency, the controller at Cleveland knew precisely the location of the flight and its position in relation to the closest airport for an emergency landing.

"Are you returning to Detroit Metro?" asked the controller.

"Negative," replied the captain. "I want to get into an airport that's in the open—where's one open?"

He was informed that the nearest airport, Windsor International, 4 miles north of the flight's position, was operating and its runway and approach lights were in operation.

Less than one minute had transpired since the crisis had developed. In the passenger compartment all hell had broken loose. When the cabin had depressurized, paper, magazines, coffee cups, hats, coats, shawls, small baggage, and pillows had flown around as if twisted by a hurricane. The lights had gone out, a thick, smoky mist filled the cabin, and the awful noise of screeching air pierced the eardrums of the passengers. Blowing horns could be heard from the cockpit. Added to these terrifying sounds were people's screams as the floor sank into the cargo hatch below. Many of the passengers thought that the airliner was in its death throes. They were close to being right.

On the flight deck, a deeply concerned Captain McCormick elected to return to Detroit Metropolitan Airport, from which he had taken off five minutes before the trouble began. He was not familiar with Windsor, but he knew the Detroit airport had extra-long runways for an emergency landing, and boasted excellent safety facilities for rescuing passengers in case of a fire-followed crash landing.

At once a general emergency was proclaimed at Detroit Metropolitan Airport. All aircraft heading for the busy terminus were diverted into holding patterns in central Michigan and southwestern Ontario. All takeoffs were stopped, and aircraft at the boarding stations turned off their engines. Passengers were informed there would be delays because of "traffic." Friends and relatives who had so recently waved farewell to the passengers of Flight 96 were driving away from the crowded parking lot that lined the inner circle of the giant airport. They had no knowledge that the flight was trying to return.

At twenty-five minutes and twenty-five seconds after nine o'clock, Cleveland Center ordered: "Right turn heading to one eight zero, maintain ten thousand, go ahead."

When the center asked for further details, they were told: "We have a control problem: We have no rudder." Unable to turn the jet to the right or to the left, they indeed had a control problem.

Cleveland at once ordered Flight 96 down to 9,000 feet for an instrument landing approach on Runway 3, where equipment would be standing by. Runway 3, a north-south ribbon of concrete, was the most direct approach for the severely crippled aircraft.

"We'll let down slowly," answered the captain, mindful of the 300,000 pounds of fuel in the wings which he would not have time to dump. In any case, flight crews are reluctant to dump fuel after the signal of a fire warning. The weight of the fuel therefore was an added hazard to the landing.

To compound the situation, the wind was changing from the east to southeast and the cloud layer at 4,500 feet was now thickening. Visibility had dropped from 2 miles to 1.5 miles due to an increase of industrial smoke typical of the Detroit airport region.

Speeding into rescue positions along either side of the runway were two Yankee Walters 2,500-gallon foam tankers, another 3,000-gallon foam vehicle, one light rescue truck with 1,000 pounds of powder chemicals, one 750-gallon water pumper, a rescue van, and the firefighters augmented by airport supervisory people. This collection of firefighting and rescue equipment is typical of major metropolitan airports only. The dry powder chemical is similar to baking soda and is spewed at the rate of 35 pounds a second to cool the heat of the flames and retard the spreading of the fire. Its prime use is to keep the heat of fire from the fuselage of the aircraft. Huge quantities of foam then cover the flames to deprive the fire of its required oxygen.

Captain McCormick squeezed his microphone button and continued his conversation with Cleveland Center: "Ah, we've got a problem. I got a hole in the cabin. I think we lost number-two engine—we've got a jammed rudder—and we need to get down."

"Turn farther right to two zero zero."

"I have no rudder control whatsoever, so our turns are gonna have to be slow and cautious."

"Understand," replied Cleveland Center.

The co-pilot belatedly informed the captain and the second officer that he was getting a certain amount of heading control by jockeying the engines on the right and left wings, reducing power on the right and speeding up the power on the left to provide a slow turn to the right and conversely to turn the aircraft to the left. While he was improving on this system, Cleveland requested that the flight descend to 5,000 feet in addition to reporting every second or so the conditions of the descent and the responses from the flying controls.

The flaps on the wings were lowered to a position of 15 degrees. The extension of the flaps increased the area of the wings to provide a greater lifting surface at lower speeds.

The aircraft was further instructed to descend to 3,000 feet and report at that time. This would place it beneath the cloud cover and eliminate the bouncing up and down associated with flying in cloud turbulence.

Captain McCormick was feeling his way toward the unseen runway, jockeying the engines, working the yoke back and forth, studying the responses of the Jumbo to this system of descending. Ordinarily descent is accomplished by the automatic pilot in conjunction with sensing equipment at the approach end of the active runway. Seldom do pilots revert to this "seat of the pants" flying, which was normal during the early days of aviation and during single-engine training flights.

As the aircraft ponderously approached the airport, the flight attendants were busy activating emergency landing procedures necessary for all passengers to obey: seats were returned to their upright position, pillows placed in front of the heads, eyeglasses and false teeth removed, seat belts tightened as firmly as possible around the hips, arms folded in front of the chest so that forearms were braced against the seat backs immediately ahead, and heads bent down to prevent neck snapping. All loose objects were stuffed under the seats, small children were placed on parents' knees, and pillows and blankets were placed in front of them to absorb any shock. All was now ready and the passengers and flight attendants waited nervously for the landing.

"We've got a nice rate of descent. Even if we have to touch down this way, we're doing well," commented the co-pilot to relieve the tension on the flight deck. Whether the crew survived the emergency landing or not, these comments would be preserved on a crash-protected tape recorder to be played back later by investigators.

The radio crackled: "American 96, this is Detroit."

Ninety-Six was now under the direct control of Detroit's Approach Control, where, in a darkened room, controllers were watching the plane on their radarscopes and talking it down on a radar glidepath to the runway.

"Loud and clear," replied the co-pilot. "We're through three thousand."

The Approach Control supervisor told Captain McCormick to maintain an altitude of 3,000 feet until such time as a shallow right turn would align the jet with the row of runway lights. More than a score of other aircraft were within radio range and every pilot was listening to the drama.

"Gimme the gear," ordered Captain McCormick, and the thump of the giant undercarriage falling into position could be clearly heard over the open radio system. The speed of the two engines was increased slightly to compensate for the added drag of the undercarriage.

"I'm going to start slowing her down—gimme twenty-two on the flaps," the captain instructed his co-pilot.

The lowering of the flaps into a position of 22 degrees down provided even greater wing area.

The controller called: "American ninety-six, you're two and a half miles from the marker, contact the tower on one-two-one-point-one and good night."

Co-pilot Whitney turned his radio dial to the assigned frequency for the control tower.

It was now forty-two minutes and twenty seconds past nine o'clock. The control tower informed the flight that it was cleared to land. The controllers could see its brilliant pattern of landing lights and flashing red identification signals in the haze.

"Give me thirty-five flaps," ordered the captain. Whitney pulled the lever to set the flaps full down and replied an okay. The speed was approximately 125 knots.

With the suddenness of an opening curtain, the flashing strobe lights appeared in the near distance and then the running lights emerged and two long lines of flashing red emergency lights. Detroit was ready.

"I have no rudder to straighten it out with when she hits," the captain blurted out. The DC-10 zoomed over the perimeter lights and settled toward the concrete just ahead and below.

"Okay," gasped the co-pilot. "Engines off at your discretion." They were over the last of the approach lights.

"Shut em down!" yelled the captain, raising his voice for the first time since the trouble started. The inertia and speed of the jet would carry it to the threshold of the runway.

Unable to flare its nose to the sky because of the damage to the controls, it struck the runway solidly and without a bounce, and careened forward at over 100 miles an hour until the reverse thrust of the two wing engines slowed it down. The aircraft then ran off the runway with fire and rescue apparatus in close pursuit. It finally came to a halt in the grass and the crew gave one great sigh of relief.

As the DC-10 was rolling along the concrete, several more ceiling panels fell on the passengers. When the aircraft came to a full stop, the cabin lights went out. Emergency exit doors on the mid-sides of the aircraft opened, but two exits at the rear could not be used because of the collapsed floors. The emergency evacuation signal lights were activated on the flight deck since they had not turned on automatically when the cabin lights went out. Evacuation slides deployed automatically, as they are supposed to do. But they took a full seventeen seconds to be inflated, a length of time that might have been fatal in the case of a crash followed by fire. Two of the slides fell inside the cabin and had to be kicked out.

The passengers got out quickly, although two elderly ladies had to be helped through the exits and one passenger's path was obstructed by a ceiling panel. Most of them were unable to maintain a feet-first position while sliding down the center of the double-occupancy surface chutes, and injuries were sustained by nine passengers at the bottom of the slides.

Meanwhile, 20 miles away, Ontario Provincial Police officers had arrived on the scene in answer to Sante Facca's call. Excitement and curiosity increased as they walked out to inspect the object partially imbedded in the earth.

A concentration of flashlights revealed a dark-colored coffin inside the metal-strapped wooden case. The lower part had broken open, allowing the legs of an elderly woman to show. Sante and the police were amazed to observe such slight damage to the coffin, which had plummeted from the clouds.

Across the highway, where the first mysterious thump had been heard, police found a large piece of shiny metal, not unlike aluminum but heavier. They could not explain the connection between the metal object and the coffin, and they were not to know until some time later that it was part of the American DC-10.

That piece of metal was about to become the number-one exhibit in the case of the DC-10, a problem that would be probed for many months before being revealed by the safety team already en route to Detroit to determine the cause of the accident.

6

The Safety Board Enters the Case

Isolate the problem and have it corrected before similar troubles appear in other DC-10s.

That was the goal of the Safety Board team that descended on Detroit to pinpoint a design failure that had almost become a catastrophe. In June of 1972 there were fewer than a hundred DC-10s in world service, but there would soon be more than four hundred of these Jumbos—all of them concealing a serious and possibly lethal problem.

The Safety Board's function in relation to aviation is to determine the probable cause of a fatal accident. There are 170 field investigators who make up twelve regional teams, and since almost all commercial airliners in the free world are designed and produced in the United States, the findings by the Board can create international ramifications because its verdicts will stand the test of court litigations. In some cases, the probable cause will have a profound effect upon foreign governments in the purchase of a new breed of airliner after the Board has discovered a design or a flight problem. Most airlines in other countries are owned by the government.

If the Board discovers that insufficiently long runways, inadequate fire and rescue services, bad weather forecasting, sloppy operations, inferior maintenance, and marginal training of flight crews have contributed in any degree to the cause of a crash or the safety of air travelers, the Board will say so, without prejudice, in its recommendations to the FAA. Little wonder it is held in such respect.

The Board is comprised of five members who are appointed by the President and confirmed by the Senate for a term of five years.

Because there is no other investigative body as sophisticated as the Safety Board anywhere in the world, it will always, upon request of foreign governments, permit "observers," who are in reality crash investigation specialists, to assist in determining the cause of major air crashes. Because it has the authority to call upon the aircraft industry and the sciences involving medicine and weather as well as the power to conduct public meetings with subpoena jurisdiction, it is almost alone in maintaining the high degree of flying efficiency and performance of U.S. and world aviation.

Time was when pilots and aircraft manufacturers as well as airport authorities took issue with the recommendations of the Safety Board, but today the industry agrees that the organization is thorough in all its investigations, and it does not exclude government agencies for their role in safety deficiencies in the over-all system.

The investigation at Detroit began with the Duralumin panel retrieved from Sante Facca's farm field near Windsor. It turned out to be one of the cargo hatches from a DC-10. There are several of these massive doors located along each side of the aircraft below the passenger cabins to receive cargo and personal baggage from the train of wagons and belt systems that form the connection between the aircraft and the baggage ramps inside the terminals. It was obvious to the team of probers who descended on the farm field that the hatch had separated from the American Airlines flight during the climb-out and the resulting loss of internal pressure had whisked the metal coffin of Edith O'Dell of Attica, New York, out of the baggage compartment like a feather in a tornado. Why it hadn't smashed into a thousand pieces when it struck the ground will forever remain a mystery.

The mystery that concerned the Safety Board, however, was

in flight. Why should a supposedly structurally sound cabin floor collapse because of depressurization caused by the cargo door failure? The investigators realized that when the hatch flew off there was an instantaneous rush of air from the passenger compartments to the baggage area to equalize the pressure. The reason that passengers seated at the rear of the aircraft had not been sucked out into space was because the collapsed floor created a barrier across the hatch opening. However, the sagging floor snapped the control cables that ran from the flight deck to the tail section.

The first question to answer was: had the cargo door been properly shut by American's cargo handlers? If it hadn't been, a red light would have showed on both the pilot's and the engineer's instrument panels and the aircraft would not have taken off until the matter was corrected.

The flight crew said that no warning lights had shown on the panels. The baggageman who had closed the aft door recalled that it had been difficult to shut but that he had finally secured it to his satisfaction because the handle fitted into its slot, which it would not have done had the door not been fully closed.

The investigating team had probed hundreds of crashes, most of them twisted and fire-ravaged piles of junk. This American DC-10 was in good condition and all parts were present to be examined. By studying the hatch and the framework in which it was enclosed, they discovered that the bolt that secured the hatch to the framework had been sheared off. This was a positive indication that the hatch had been torn off when the pressure of the cargo compartment increased as the jet ascended.

They checked the stress tests of the door fasteners and found that the assembly would withstand 6,600 pounds of pressure before failing. It was obvious that no such pressure would have built up inside the aircraft. Therefore, some other factor caused the rip-off.

As soon as this deduction had been made, the Safety Board immediately notified the FAA, and the FAA in turn telephoned all airlines using the DC-10 to have the pilots check the door latch after the baggage handlers had closed them for flight. If it was found that a hatch door would not close easily, the aircraft was to be taken out of service and inspected by the maintenance crew and corrected. This was not an order. *It was only an advisory.*

As for the catastrophic collapse of the passenger floor and its structural supports, the Safety Board was severely critical of McDonnell-Douglas: "The lack of pressure relief vents in the cargo compartment represents a significant hazard, jeopardizing the safety of the flight."

The Board then moved quickly to prevent similar accidents in the DC-10 fleet by recommending to the FAA that modifications should be made to the cargo door locking system to make it physically impossible to position the external locking handle to the normal "door locked" position unless the locking pins were fully engaged. The Board also recommended the immediate installation of relief vents between the passenger cabin and the cargo compartment to minimize the pressure on the cabin floor in the event of a sudden decompression in that area.

But under an act of Congress passed in 1958 establishing the Federal Aviation Administration, the FAA may either accept or reject recommendations from the Safety Board. It seems incredible that the FAA has such power. Because it is a large and cumbersome bureaucracy and tries to create a perfect flying system in America, it often fails due to the sheer magnitude of its responsibilities. It sets the regulations of all air commerce. It controls all navigable airspace, develops aids to all navigation and communication, regulates all civilian and military aircraft in the U.S. airspace, promulgates all safety regulations and air traffic rules, administers all airport safety regulations, tests and certifies aircraft design, and provides the certification of all aircraft for flight.

According to custom, therefore, the Safety Board's chairman, John Reed, had the vital recommendations hand-delivered to J. H. Shaffer, administrator of the FAA, on July 6, 1972.

The very next day Shaffer replied to Reed:

Dear Mr. Chairman;

This is to acknowledge your Safety Recommendations A72-97 and 98 issued on July 6, 1972, which included recommendations resulting from an inadvertent cargo door opening reported on a Douglas DC-10 airplane.

All operators of DC-10 airplanes are currently performing 100 hour functional checks on the cargo door system and will incorporate necessary modifications in accordance with McDonnell-Douglas Service Bulletins 52-57 and A52-35, within 300 hours. These modifications pertain to improvements in the inspection and operation of locking and venting mechanisms.

Additional modifications to the cargo door locking and pressurization are being considered as part of the continuing investigation effort. While a preliminary investigation indicates that it may not be feasible to provide complete venting between cabin and cargo compartment your recommendations will be considered with respect to action taken.

It was apparent from this communication that Shaffer did not agree with the Safety Board that the situation was alarming. It was in his power to ground the DC-10 immediately and remove it from commercial service until the aircraft was restructured and the cargo door and the passenger floor made fail-safe. To accomplish this task, he had to issue an airworthiness directive.

The Administrator at that moment had adequate support for such an action. His Los Angeles office had suggested to him that he issue an airworthiness directive against McDonnell-Douglas. The Los Angeles section of the FAA had evidence that McDonnell-Douglas had been aware of the cargo hatch and floor-venting problems before the Detroit crash. At that time, when the engineers began raising the pressure in the fuselage to simulate normal flying conditions, the cargo door blew off and the floor collapsed, even though the mounting increase in pressure had not reached the normal flight requirements.

A national U.S. magazine quoted a Douglas engineer as saying: "It seems to me inevitable that in the twenty years ahead of us, DC-10 cargo doors will come open and cargo compartments will experience decompression for other reasons, and I would expect this to usually result in the loss of the airplane."

When Los Angeles continued to insist on an airworthiness directive, McDonnell-Douglas appealed to Shaffer and reached what has been called a "gentleman's agreement." McDonnell-Douglas would issue a service bulletin calling for "voluntary compliance," meaning that airlines would be responsible for making changes that would ensure the safety of the doors—and those changes were expected to be nothing more than the pilot check-out. This obviously satisfied Shaffer because he never did issue an airworthiness directive.

Blandly overlooking the investigation by the Safety Board, the aircraft industry made the cargo handler at Detroit the scapegoat. Usually the baggage and cargo handlers are young men, often in their late teens or early twenties, who cannot be expected to be safety engineers or experienced mechanics qualified to decide whether or not a door is operating according to directions printed on the fuselage beside each hatch.

So it was not strange that, when the next DC-10 hatch problem occurred, McDonnell-Douglas immediately blamed a cargo handler.

7

Death Was Stalking the DC-10

Shortly before noon on the hazy spring morning of March 3, 1974, the cargo handlers at Orly International Airport near Paris shut the hatches in the belly of a Turkish Airlines DC-10 en route from Ankara to London.

There were approximately 350 passengers aboard the fully loaded airliner and most of them were delighted by the prospect of getting home to England or catching connecting flights to America. They had been waiting for days to get out of Paris but had been stymied by a strike at London's Heathrow Airport. Turkish Airlines had some 300 seats vacant for the Paris-to-London leg of its regular run and they were quickly reserved by British Airways and other airlines.

As the chimes of twelve noon reverberated over the city of gaiety, Captains Nejat Berkoz and Oral Ulusman started the triple engines of their shining new airliner and headed for the takeoff apron of the airport. Receiving an Air Traffic Control clearance for the short hop to London, the pilots brought the engines to full power. The DC-10 roared down the runway for twenty-seven seconds and lifted into the air at precisely 12:16 P.M.

One minute after takeoff the captains switched off the "No Smoking" and the "Seat Belt" signs and the passengers relaxed for a quick refreshment period before the descent into London.

At 13,000 feet above the immaculate fields of northeast France, just as the clock on the aircraft instrument panel recorded the time at 12:28 P.M., the emergency fire warning horn suddenly sounded on the flight deck. Simultaneously there was a loss of pressure in the passenger compartments. Controls to the number-two engine ceased to function. The glowing fire warning signal flashed the heart-chilling message that the flight was in critical trouble.

The pilots were immediately aware that depressurization had occurred somewhere in the passenger area, but they did not know that the rear floor had collapsed. The cabins had already filled with the flotsam of decompression—dust, fog, and flying objects.

Captains Berkoz and Ulusman were not thinking of the panic immediately behind them. Their job was to ascertain the problem and attempt to control it. They were cognizant of the sound of increased air pressure as the system automatically attempted to cope with the loss of air inside the airliner.

Captain Berkoz' first words were: "What's happened?"

His co-pilot replied: "The cabin has blown out."

"Are you sure?" asked Berkoz incredulously.

There was no answer to his query. Unknown to him, six passengers had been sucked out of the airliner and were lazily falling to oblivion. The controls of the mighty jet had now frozen. There was no time to call Orly. The job at hand was to try and save the airliner.

"Bring it up—pull her nose up," commanded Berkoz, fifty-one seconds after the alarm had issued its raucous warning.

"I can't bring her up—she doesn't respond," answered Ulusman in an anguished voice.

"Acaba nedir—nedir," sang the nervous Berkoz, parroting the well-known Turkish television commercial which asks its audience, "What is it—what is it?"

Seven seconds after his command to pull up the nose Berkoz heard the overspeed warning horn, indicating that the airliner was in a dive.

"Nothing is left," gasped the co-pilot; "we're down to seven thousand feet."

Captain Berkoz asked if there were any hydraulics left, indicating a complete loss of control.

"We have lost it," answered a voice in the confusion of horns and shrieking sounds. It may have been Erhan Ozer; it may have been the co-pilot; the noise within the cockpit was so intense that the identity of voices became impossible.

At this point more power was applied to the engines in an attempt to raise the nose of the airliner. Even with all directional controls gone, there was always the slim chance that the airliner could be leveled out either for continuing flight or for a crash landing.

"It looks like we're going to hit the ground," said Captain Berkoz in the calm manner of a professional pilot who knows that death is imminent and there is nothing left to do.

With only seconds left, Captain Berkoz uttered, "Oops." It was his last breath. One second later the airliner impacted with the earth.

A short distance away, an airport controller from Le Bourget Airport, which was once the international air capital of Paris, was driving his car along the highway in the vicinity of Roissy when he noticed the DC-10. He slowed down to watch the aircraft more closely. It was in obvious trouble. His first impression was that the aircraft was heading for the military airport at Roissy, but, collecting his thoughts, he realized it was heading in the wrong direction and descending far too fast for a landing. He saw no trailing smoke. No fire.

Then he saw it fly into the treetops. Three seconds later there was a tremendous explosion, which enveloped the Forest of Ermenonville, the favorite picnic spot of Parisians, in a mushroom of fire and thick black smoke.

Racing to the scene, the controller was met by an unbelievable spectacle of smoldering wreckage scattered for hundreds of feet, pieces of engines and aircraft parts sizzling in the new-fallen snow, which was littered with a mass of torn bodies and wreckage—a child's doll, bits of clothing, a broken watch, children's games, football sweaters—and massive blotches of red from the congealed blood in the snow. Puffs of smoke spewed upward like geysers from a netherworld. There were no survivors.

Seats and fittings had been almost totally destroyed by explosion and fire. The cockpit had been torn away at the moment of impact and, now crumpled like an accordion, faced back along the crash path. A small section of wing lay several feet away. About 300 meters rearward from the cockpit, a section of fuselage containing ten broken windows dangled from shredded trees.

Including crew members, some 347 people had died. Bodies were unrecognizable. When search teams arrived later, they faced the grisly job of scooping the remains into plastic bags. Identification of the mangled corpses was impossible. They were removed to mortuary chapels at Senlis and Meaux.

President Pompidou expressed his regrets to Queen Elizabeth because of the large number of British subjects on the plane. In Turkey, President Fahri Koruturk announced a national day of mourning. The crash was the worst in aviation history.

While official regrets were being expressed by France and Turkey, their authorities, without any evidence whatsoever, called the crash an act of sabotage. They "found" witnesses who swore they saw an explosion in the air before the plane went down. Some claimed to have seen fire and smoke trailing from the aft section of the plane. Officials blandly ignored the eyewitness report of the airport controller, who had spent a third of his adult life observing airplanes. They also overlooked the fact that six passengers had been blown out of the aircraft 9 miles behind the crash, a sure indication there had been a pressurization failure.

A number of American newspapers hinted at the similarity of the Windsor flying coffin episode and the expulsion of passengers from a DC-10, both of which happened at approximately the same height. But the hue and cry for identification of the American and British victims and the continual assertions from the French press and authorities that sabotage was the cause led those newspapers that noted a grave similarity between Windsor and Paris to be caught up in the confusion, and Windsor was forgotten.

But the FAA and McDonnell-Douglas Aircraft didn't believe it was sabotage, even though some of the aircraft company's public relations mouthpieces were parroting the charges. The British Broadcasting Corporation went so far as to hint that various anti-Turkish elements who had been active in the Mideast were implicated.

A French military bomb squad had been unable to find evidence of an explosion during preliminary investigation because the wreckage was so widely scattered and the task of identifying parts of bodies to form a single victim was impossible. The British Air Ministry offered to send in a team of forensic specialists who were experts in the identification of fire and crash victims, but the French refused this assistance. Not only did they not know the number of persons aboard the flight, they had no record of the names of persons who had bought tickets or had been transferred to the flight by British Airways.

Airlines do not maintain a record of passengers' names and the seat numbers to which they are assigned. It would be a relatively simple procedure to do so, and in case of a crash, it would be a major help in identifying bodies. The six bodies that had plummeted to the ground before the crash were quickly identified, but the authorities had no way of knowing where they had been seated in the aircraft. If they had been assigned numbers before they boarded, Air Ministry experts would have been able to pinpoint the area of depressurization and would have discovered that it occurred in the same location as that in the DC-10 over Windsor. Not having this information permitted the guesswork to continue in Paris while FAA and McDonnell-Douglas awaited the awful moment of truth.

A serious lack of command hampered the investigation right from the beginning, and a desperate situation had developed. Before army units arrived to protect the area from vandalism, which is a common occurrence after air crashes, souvenir hunters carried away important human documentation and bits of valuable aircraft wreckage. Clothing was stolen. Personal effects that normally scatter in profusion at the initial impact were missing. In addition, human teeth, which are often the best means of identification through dental charts, had dissolved into dust from the force of the crash and the fire-followed explosion.

While Britons and Americans continued to clamor for the names of the victims, the theft of purses, watches, wallets, belt buckles, scraps of clothing, rings, and other items of jewelry left the French identification specialists without any clues whatsoever. Next of kin of missing persons flew to Paris in an effort to identify scraps of personal effects or isolated birthmarks or other characteristics on bits of preserved human scraps. But to no avail. The French were now trying to identify victims by obtaining the names of persons who should have by now returned to their homes in the United States and Great Britain, trying to relate them to those who could have been on the flight.

In attempting to learn the names of those who had checked in at the Turkish Airlines counter from canceled British Airways flights, the French Air Ministry discovered such a jumble of nationalities and names, passport forgeries, and phony marriages, as well as a new habit of name-exchanging to cover up vacations, that trying to form any kind of list became impossible.

Passports found at the scene and sent quickly to Scotland Yard in London were found, in some cases, to be faked and in other cases to have been borrowed. The rightful owners, who were at home, were aware of the Paris disaster but unwilling to come forward and identify the persons to whom they had loaned their documents. To do so would have meant a possible jail term. A reorganization of immigration and security was immediately ordered by the British government.

Some couples traveling as man and wife were not married, and this posed more problems for the British, who then had to try to track down errant husbands and illicit relationships. The crash provoked a national scandal.

Three weeks after the accident, only twenty-one death certificates had been issued by the French government. One man who had been listed as dead showed up to explain that his girl friend always carried his passport because she liked his photograph in it.

Angry British families who were next of kin of missing persons, now presumed dead, demanded that the French government return the bodies to England for burial. The French refused because they could not tell British corpses from any others.

To compound the mix-up even further, the French have a law that will not permit unidentified human remains to be buried alongside an identified person. The French were in a quandary. Following an air disaster of such magnitude, the usual way to dispose of the dead is in a common grave. After weeks of vainly trying to identify the remaining bodies, it was decided to bury them all together in a common grave and ship the bodies of the six identified persons back to their families.

Among those who were known to have boarded the aircraft was Dr. Wayne Wilcox, forty-one-year-old cultural attaché to the U. S. Embassy in London. A former political science chairman of Columbia University, Wilcox was traveling with his wife Ouida, who had been until recently the chairman of London's Southeast Shakespeare Festival, and the two eldest of their four children, Kailan and Clark Wilcox.

John Hanessian, of the National Science Foundation of Washington, D.C., was also a victim, as were four leading London fashion models, eighteen members of the Suffolk rugby team, and some two hundred other Britons. The calamity also claimed the life of Thomas P. Wright, a member of the brokerage firm of Merrill, Lynch, in New York City. His wife Fay and their children also died. A number of prominent Japanese perished and were buried together with Turkish emigrants bound for a new life in America.

The French belatedly announced that there were no chemical deposits on the cargo door found near the six bodies 9 miles from the crash site. Nor had there been any cordite deposits in any of the flesh specimens or, in fact, in any part of the wreckage. It was logical to assume, at last, that no bomb explosion had occurred on the DC-10.

Following this announcement, President Sanford Douglas of McDonnell-Douglas Aircraft made a statement to the annual meeting of the corporation being held in St. Louis. He declared that it was inexcusable that a French baggage handler in Paris, "who was responsible for closing the cargo door" of the Turkish flight, couldn't read English, the language in which the instructions were printed.

Not a few must have wondered how many baggage handlers in Germany, Pakistan, Turkey, Algeria, and scores of other countries of the world knew how to read English.

Now it became obvious that the FAA was thinking about the near-disaster back at Windsor. After receiving from the French Air Ministry the details of the cargo hatch damage, which included the shearing of the lockpins similar to the occurrence in Windsor, the FAA acted—not with an airworthiness directive as might be expected after the worst crash in history, but with a bulletin that protected McDonnell-Douglas and placed the onus for the cargo hatch operation and inspection squarely on the airlines.

Not only did the FAA duck the censuring of the manufacturer, it continued to insist that the cause of the problem was the improper shutting of the cargo doors, despite the fact hat pilots had not been made aware of the siutation by the red instrument panel lights.

The following was issued to all operators of the DC-10s:

1. Prior to further flight, unless already accomplished, perform the modifications and functional checks related below as follows:

A. Install viewing window in all cargo doors. Install placards and perform functional checks of door system and operation with McDonnell-Douglas Service Bulletin A52-35, dated 19 June 1972.

B. Modify the cargo door latch actuator wiring in accordance with McDonnell-Douglas Service Bulletin 52-57, dated 30 May 1972, or later F.A.A. approved revisions.

C. Except for those aircraft which may have been modified in accordance with McDonnell-Douglas Service Bulletin 52-49, dated 25 October 1973, or later F.A.A. Approved revisions, replace strike plate and adjust the switches on all forward, center and aft cargo doors and install a support and plate on the aft cargo door in accordance with McDonnell-Douglas Service

Bulletin 52-37, dated 3 July 1972, or later F.A.A. approved revision.

2. Prior to each flight, a crew member must check each cargo door as follows:

A. Ensure that the cargo restraint curtain is in its proper position.

B. Ensure that no foreign matter is in the exposed door locking mechanism.

C. Ensure that the locking mechanisms are in their proper positions.

D. Accomplish a visual inspection through the inspection port and for locking pin placement.

E. Ensure all cargo door warning lights are extinguished prior to taxiing.

3. If any abnormalities in pressurization are observed during flight immediately depressurize the aircraft and land at the nearest suitable airport.

4. The checks required by these Airworthiness Directives are to be accomplished by flight crew, notwithstanding any requirement of Federal Aviation Regulations.

Simultaneous with the issuance of this Directive, inspectors assigned to U.S. DC-10 operators will institute action to amend approved air carrier training programs to assure flight crew members are thoroughly familiar with and indoctrinated in the operation of locked cargo doors.

Between the Windsor affair and the French accident, inspectors at the manufacturing centers of two other Jumbos, the Lockheed 1011 and the Boeing 747, discovered that the venting systems in the rear cabin floor areas were similar to those in the DC-10, although no catastrophic collapse of these floors had been reported.

The similarity was so impressive that after the Paris crash the Lockheed 1011 and the Boeing 747 were included in an FAA order to modify the venting systems and beef up the rear passenger floors.

After Paris, airlines using the Jumbos began filling all forward and middle seats before placing passengers in the rearmost seats because of the fear that the aft floors would collapse.

Now they had a directive to modify the system—but the kits

would not be delivered to their maintenance staffs until the fall of 1975, and it would be well into 1976, and perhaps beyond, before all the floors were strengthened and the venting systems increased. Until every Jumbo was modified, passengers would be riding on luck.

A newly appointed FAA administrator, James E. Dow, in announcing the order, estimated that the U.S. fleet costs alone would reach $43 million, plus an additional $18 million in lost revenues for the period when the Jumbos were out of passenger service being beefed up.

United Airlines estimated that to comply with structural changes in their fleet of eighteen 747s would cost a minimum of $1,100,000 and require one thousand man-hours per aircraft to fix. But the industry thought these figures too conservative and that many millions more would be added to the bill. Foreign operators were expected to follow the FAA rulings—but were *not required* to do so. Air France announced that FAA directives would be followed to the letter, but that it would take some six months to receive the modification kits. The British Civil Aviation Authority issued similar orders to British Airways' 747s and Lockheed 1011s and Laker Airways' DC-10s. It was announced, also, that Air France, Lufthansa, Alitalia, Iberia, and Sabena would make the changes with a maintenance pool system, once the kits were available.

The final irony of the floor problems occurred when airlines were informed in mid-1975 that they would have to bear the costs of modifying the venting systems in both the Boeing 747 and the DC-10. Not only that, but DC-10s coming off the assembly lines up until January 1976 would *not* be equipped with the suggested modifications.

The cost was not estimated by Boeing or Douglas, but airlines, already squeezed dry by mounting operation problems, saw millions of dollars looming like a nightmare over the labor and parts costs of the modifications. How many, therefore, would rush pell-mell into the program to protect the flying public? It was anybody's guess.

Lockheed made no decision as to who was going to pay for the beefing-up of the 1011. But, said one official of an airline using the Lockheeds, "I'll bet a buck we'll have to cough up the money."

McDonnell-Douglas announced at this time that manufacturing plans as well as testing platforms had been completed for the structural modifications in the DC-10s soon to be traveling along the assembly lines. New designs had been approved for the additional venting between the cabins and the cargo space as well as "some localized structural modifications."

The manufacturing rate of modification kits for DC-10s already in world service or being prepared for delivery at Douglas plants had struck a snag. It did not seem possible to Douglas that enough of the kits could be made available and installed by the deadline of December 31, 1977, set by the benevolent FAA.

In the meantime, structurally deficient Jumbos would continue in service into 1978 and everyone would just have to keep his fingers crossed.

8

One of Our Passengers Is Missing

Although the DC-10 is a delightful plane to fly, big and roomy, quiet but with a feeling of tremendous power, it started its career, like many new breeds of aircraft, with serious problems that were reported by the Safety Board to the FAA soon after the plane was introduced into service in 1970 and prior to the Paris disaster.

If ever a plane should have been grounded for bad performance, the DC-10 was it. The crash at Paris was the second fatal accident. The first one involved National Airline's Flight 27 on November 3, 1973, during a scheduled run from Miami to San Francisco with intermediate stops at New Orleans, Houston, and Las Vegas.

Ordinarily, this is a delightful flight when the weather is clear. The climbout over Florida greenery opens onto the panorama of the Gulf of Mexico curving along the northwest coast of Florida into Alabama and Louisiana. Outbound from New Orleans the flight cruises at lower altitudes because of the short hop to Houston, but after that, it ascends almost to the extreme limit of its capability, where the air is royal blue and icy cold, with temperatures normally at 30 or more below zero.

The weather that late afternoon in early November was typical. As the flight crossed above the border of Texas and New Mexico, heavy clouds had formed far below. The DC-10 was zipping through the thin air at a ground speed of approximately 530 miles an hour, or 257 knots. The calculated elapsed time between Houston and Las Vegas was two hours and forty-nine minutes, and the flight was right on the button.

Captain William R. Broocke, fifty-four, was in command. A veteran pilot, he had chalked up thousands of flying hours in such famous planes as the C-46, Lockheed Lodestar, Convair-340 and -440, DC-6, Lockheed Electra, Boeing 727, and DC-10. He had become a captain in the DC-10 on May 13, 1972, and had flown 801 hours in the Jumbo, bringing his total to almost 22,000 hours of professional flying. It was a good thing he was aboard. When the DC-10 runs into trouble, a superb pilot in command sometimes makes the difference between life and death.

His first officer was Eddie Saunders, thirty-three, with an impressive career of multi-engine flying. He had completed his DC-10 training in September 1972, and was assigned as first officer of the aircraft in April 1973. He had accumulated 7,086 flying hours, of which 445 hours were in the DC-10. His last proficiency test had been just thirty-eight days before this flight.

Seated before the vast array of glowing lights and instruments of the master panel was Flight Engineer Golden W. Hanks, fifty-five, whom everyone called "Goldie." He had accumulated 17,814 flight hours, of which more than 1,200 were in the DC-10. There was no doubt that the three men comprising the flight crew had an impressive flying record.

Tucked away in the entrails of the mighty Jumbo were two important systems: the flight data system, to record the behavior of the airliner, and the voice recorder, which recorded the voices of the flight crew, to be used only in case of an accident. The voice recorder was working. But the flight data recorder was not.

National Airlines maintenance procedure requires that data recorders be tested after every two thousand hours of operation. The records of the system that was aboard Flight 27 revealed that the last test was on July 30, 1973. The results of this check-out were noted in the maintenance book: "Failed test—5 of 11 failed speed checks—other checks unreliable." Maintenance personnel had tested the flight recorder with electronic equipment. When the system did not pass the test, the recorder was replaced with other stock units and these units were tested. When these units also failed, it was *assumed* that the test equipment was faulty and the original units were reinstalled.

Goldie Hanks was intent on his instrumental panel as the hands of the clock ticked past four o'clock. Sunshine was flooding the cockpit with brilliant rainbows of color. The climb from Houston had been made with the automatic pilot system. The automatic throttle system was feeding the correct amount of fuel to the three mighty General Electric engines. As the airliner leveled out at 39,000 feet and reported its height to Albuquerque Air Traffic Control, the automatic throttle was disengaged and the pilot manually set his cruising speed at 257 knots. The automatic pilot would follow precisely the programmed navigational pathway.

At twenty minutes after four, when the aircraft was over Socorro, New Mexico, Captain Broocke re-engaged the automatic throttle at the target of 257 knots. At this point Goldie Hanks performed a failure analysis on the automatic throttle system. Circuit breakers were pulled to determine if the disconnection would affect the automatic throttle. The response apparently satisfied Broocke. But the two men had triggered an action of which they were unaware. The disconnection of the circuit breakers permitted the auto throttles to advance out of control to beyond their normal limits.

Thirty-six seconds after pulling the circuit breakers on the automatic throttle system, the flight crew heard a muffled explosion.

"What was that?" demanded Captain Broocke.

There was no immediate answer as the captain and his engineer scanned the instrument panels before them. First Officer Saunders was back in the passenger section. If there was conversation after this, there is no record of it, due to the sounds of rushing air taking precedence over all other sounds.

Number-three engine on the right wing had broken up and had splattered the fuselage with a curtain of super-hot missiles.

Turbine blades traveling at speeds as high as the speed of sound slammed into the passenger area of the plane and continued on through into the number-one engine area of the left wing.

With the sound of a thousand explosions, the passenger compartment decompressed. The cockpit began to vibrate violently. Captain Broocke pushed the button that activates an emergency signal on the radar screen being watched by the controller at Albuquerque Air Traffic Control. The noise inside the aircraft made it impossible to carry on radio conversation. But the controller knew what the flashing message beside the number NA-27 meant. *Trouble!* Captain Broocke, not as yet aware of what had caused his problem, pushed the nose of the DC-10 toward the ground and at 5,000 feet a minute dived toward Albuquerque.

If there was apprehension on the flight deck, there was absolute panic in the passenger cabins. Smoke filled the cavernous tunnel. The banshee shriek of air mixed with the screams of passengers and the swirling mass of pillows, papers, purses, handbags, napkins, glasses, and direction card reading "What to Do in an Emergency." Co-pilot Eddie Saunders clawed his way forward to reach the flight deck. As he opened the door, gasping for air, Goldie Hanks leaned back from his seat and looked into the passenger section. All he could see was blue-gray smoke. He looked at his panel. The fire warning light was pulsing. The aircraft was shaking violently and the waving needles of the instrument dials disclosed that a succession of failures was occurring throughout the flight system.

Inside the plunging DC-10 many masks failed to drop. In fact, those that fell or were pulled from the compartments took anywhere from a few seconds to over three minutes to be available for use. Some of the passengers did not know how to work the equipment. They pulled the masks from their compartments and leaned forward toward them. Consequently, a string that activates the oxygen-making equipment was not activated and these masks joined the others in not supplying oxygen. Other passengers stopped using the masks, either because they could discern no oxygen flow or the reservoir bags did not inflate. This caused them to believe the equipment was defective. All they had to do was pull the lanyard between the mask and its container. But passengers are not carefully instructed to do this. They do not realize, therefore, that an oxygen mask when it falls must be pulled sharply to the mouth or the equipment will not work.

The failure to receive oxygen at heights above 25,000 feet will render an adult person unconscious in twelve to fifteen seconds. However, air trapped within the large passenger compartment of the aircraft will help sustain consciousness for about one minute, and in rare cases, where there has been no physical activity or extreme mental anguish that would cause the heart to beat at twice its normal rate, unconsciousness will not become evident for about two minutes.

Frightened stewardesses, grabbing at dangling oxygen masks for quick deep whiffs to keep them conscious, moved along the aisles from row to row, pulling down masks and clapping them over passengers' faces. Ten passengers were already unconscious from lack of oxygen. Ten others were overcome by smoke in the front section and had collapsed in their seats.

So great was the turmoil and the lack of visibility in the cabin, none of the stewardesses noticed that the depressurization's cyclonic winds had rushed toward a broken window adjacent to seat 17-H where Bethlehem shipyard machinist G. F. Gardner, of Beaumont, Texas, was seated.

In a flash, the curved 16-by-10 inch pane was sucked into space. The escaping air from the cabin grabbed at Gardner and lifted him bodily from his slackened seat belt, jamming him against the open window. Nearby passengers, noticing with horror that Gardner was being slowly sucked into the window opening, risked their lives to unsnap their safety belts and grab him; first about the waist, then the hips, and finally his legs and feet. The effort was in vain. Gardner was drawn through the window to fall toward the ground some 30,000 feet below.

Back in the lower galley of the DC-10, two stewardesses had been seated in the jump seats facing the elevator doors. They had heard a "very loud" explosion in that part of the aircraft. There was a surge of air toward the rear of the galley. The doors to the service cart storage area flew open and the carts moved into the galley. The food delivery elevator dropped to the floor from above and the doors opened.

Wide-eyed with dismay, the two girls looked for their supplemental oxygen but noticed that the masks had not fallen. They were stood up then and reached for the portable oxygen supply that was stored behind the escape ladder. Before they could reach the equipment, they slumped to the floor, unconscious.

At three seat locations the oxygen generators were pulled from their mountings and the hot cylinders, normally protected by heavy insulation within the mountings, fell on two passengers, severely burning them. When the flight attendant pulled the cylinder to a safer place, they also were burned. The temperature of the cylinders runs as high as 547 degrees Fahrenheit.

On the flight deck, Captain Broocke could not establish contact with the High Altitude Air Traffic Control Center located southwest of Albuquerque. This was one of hundreds of remote centers across the country concerned with keeping transcontinental and other long-distance flights on specified corridors at the upper extremes of the flight levels. Nor could the controller at High Altitude reach the flight, but he was aware that National was in trouble. The tiny blip of light on his radar screen showing the echo of the aircraft was accompanied by a small transponder that showed the identity of the flight, NA 27. When Captain Broocke pushed his emergency button the rectangle began to pulsate and emitted a squawking sound that alerted the controller to the emergency.

At 4:39 P.M. the controller of High Altitude saw the emergency signal of the transponder on the radar screen and attempted to raise the flight, but there was no response, indicating there was a transmitter or receiver failure somewhere in the radio communications system.

Concerned that the failure might have been in his own transmitter, the controller called American Airlines Flight 54, which was in the scope at the time, and asked if the signal was clear and recognizable.

"Five by five," answered American, which in communications jargon means loud and clear.

The controller tried again to reach Flight 27 but received an answer instead from another National flight, number 22, passing across the control area.

"Is there any chance of you raising National 27—he's on three-five-oh-five frequency?" asked the worried controller.

"Okay . . . and if I get him, what then?"

"He's squawking an emergency in the sector above us—thirty-seven-thirty-five [altitude] and right now he's at your twelve o'clock position—position forty miles and he's north-westbound."

Then the High Altitude controller called the Albuquerque West Area Air Traffic Control Center and asked: "Do you see a mayday forty-five miles southwest of Albuquerque?"

"Yes."

"Okay, that's a National aircraft, a heavy DC-10—we can't talk to him—he's squawking emergency—he's supposed to be going to Winslow—it doesn't look like he's going that way . . . he might . . ."

"Looks like he's in a right turn."

"Yeah. You'd better keep everything out of the way—I don't know what his altitude is or where he is going."

"All right," replied Albuquerque West.

At 4:41 P.M., High Altitude, still worried, then called Approach Control at Albuquerque asking if this center had established contact with the troubled flight, and received a negative answer.

"All right then," replied High Altitude. "He's a DC-10—at the present time, he's about forty-five to fifty southwest of Albuquerque VORTAC [radio range] . . . er . . . he's changed his emergency squawk and we can't talk to him . . . he seems to be in a right turn."

"Okay, he's a DC-10."

"Yeah."

Five seconds after this conversation the other National flight was able to make contact with Flight 27 and this radio transmission was established: "Okay . . . National twenty-two . . .

I'm executing an emergency descent . . . We've lost number-three engine and we're badly rolling to the right . . . We have a moderate . . . er . . . shaking . . . We're in turbulence now . . . Would you inform Southwest Center, please."

"Yes sir, we're talking to the center ourselves."

"Abandon the airways . . . we're down at . . . er . . . one three point five right now [13,500 feet] and we're going to take her down to about ten thousand . . . We're shaking pretty badly . . . unable to shut down number-three engine . . . We've got the handle off but we can't get the fuel lever down —can't stop the fuel to the damaged engine."

National 22 instantly called High Altitude and reported the emergency descent being made by Flight 27 (to an emergency airport at Winslow) and also the fact that the aircraft was shaking badly. Albuquerque Approach Control cut in to suggest that the stricken flight should fly through to Albuquerque, even though it meant another 40 to 50 miles, because emergency equipment there was excellent.

National Flight 22 called Flight 27 and asked Captain Broocke where he intended to land, the Winslow emergency field or elsewhere. He replied: "I prefer Albuquerque right now —that's all I can do—we've got her slowed down . . . er . . . pretty good—and I'll give you an estimate in a few minutes."

"Okay, I've already contacted the center for you . . . I advised them you're making an emergency descent to ten thousand feet . . . I advised them of your condition . . . We'll keep in touch with the center and with you . . . Don't shift frequencies."

Captain Broocke replied with urgency in his voice: "Okay, give us a heading . . . We need it immediately . . . We're getting no navigational facilities right now." This indicated that the radio electrical system had failed and the flight instruments were not working.

"To where?"

"To Albuquerque airport."

By using a relay system between ground radar controllers at various locations, National's Flight 22 juggled a number of frequency changes so that the Albuquerque approach controller could contact the stricken aircraft directly and guide its pilots to the runway, already lined with the first of a large collection of rescue and fire equipment.

At 4:45 P.M. Approach made its first call on the new frequency: "National twenty-seven, this is Albuquerque Approach Control, I am reading you loud and clear . . . How do you hear me?"

"Okay. Loud and clear, Albuquerque. Go ahead."

"National twenty-seven . . . fly heading of zero eight zero . . . Descend at your discretion for vectors left . . . runway two six . . . zero one."

In the lovely blue sky of southern New Mexico, Captain Broocke and his fellow officers of the flight deck could not see the ground because of a cloud deck. Sight of the ground always gives crew and passengers a reassuring feeling when an aircraft is in trouble. And Flight 27 was indeed in trouble. It was bucking in turbulence, caused by the updraft of winds in the mountainous regions of the Rockies, and the hydraulics of the plane that operate the up and down attitude were not responding to the controls of the cockpit.

As if Captain Broocke didn't have enough to worry about at this time, he received a call from Albuquerque that there was another aircraft ahead of him at 5 miles and slightly above his altitude.

When an emergency is declared by a control center, all aircraft in the vicinity are ordered to turn away and leave the way clear for the approach of the stricken plane. For a control center to have injected the report of another aircraft ahead at this crucial time was an indication that a full understanding of an emergency may not have been specifically understood by ground controllers.

"Okay," replied Captain Broocke. "We're at eleven thousand and let us know if he gets real close and then we'll make a turn."

The controller was most reassuring: "You're okay—he'll pass to your left and no problems."

The National crew breathed a sigh of relief.

"This is National twenty-seven . . . We're definitely declaring an emergency . . . We want all your gear out there . . . Our cabin is filled with smoke . . . We're losing pressure with the number-one hydraulic system and . . . er . . . we want everything there . . . we want a straight in as quick as we can."

Although Runway 35 was directly ahead of the airliner, it was only 10,000 feet long, and the controller, thinking of the problems of landing a Jumbo without hydraulics, recommended the longer Runway 26, even thought it meant a left-hand turn. Finally Captain Broocke answered: "Okay."

"How many people you got on board?"

"Stand by . . . er . . . a hundred and fifteen . . . and say the range for us, please."

"You're sixteen miles southwest of the airport now."

"Okay . . . we're out at ninety-two hundred [feet] and just coasting on down."

"You should be able to see the airport now . . . We got the runway two six lights on . . . Let me know when you have them in sight at twelve o'clock at fourteen miles." He continued his conversation with the flight, as there was much more work to be done before it was on the ground.

There was another problem. Albuquerque is surrounded by mountain ranges, which have to be cleared before planes can make their descent into the airport. In case of a western heading, however, the descent in clear weather can be made more rapidly over a pass through the Sandia Mountains. Captain Broocke would have to be close to the mountains to make his swing and the controller was watching on his radar.

He decided to call the flight as a precautionary move: "National twenty-seven . . . there's mountains ten miles east of Albuquerque . . . You'll be making a five-mile base leg [turn] to two six . . . no more . . . no further east than that."

"Okay—and be advised, sir, we'll probably be evacuating personnel when we get on the deck."

"How much fuel on board?"

"We've got about thirty-five to forty thousand pounds."

"Okay. You're now six miles southwest of the airport on a downwind . . . I'll go ahead and keep you on this frequency until final approach . . . turn left now to three five zero."

"Okay. Three five zero."

"Turn further left . . . three two zero . . . Descend to seven thousand . . . Turn left heading two six zero . . . You're turning in on the five-mile final now to Runway two-six and you're cleared to land."

"Be advised, sir, we with . . . er . . . stewardess on board with a broken leg . . . and we don't know what else is damaged right now if you can hear me."

"Okay," signed off Approach Control.

Captain Broocke could see the airport ahead now and he eased the stricken Jumbo into a shallow left turn to line up for the landing. Strobe approach lights were flashing and beyond them, on either side of the ribbon of concrete, the flashing red lights of emergency vehicles appeared like impatient sentinels.

When the captain was only 3 miles out he eased the nose upward slightly for the final let-down. First Officer Eddie Saunders was having problems calling out the landing procedures because his instrument panel was malfunctioning. Goldie Hanks was concerned with engine behavior and hydraulic input to the control mechanisms. Number-one engine was slipping.

When the lever was activated to lower the wheels for landing, it failed to operate. The wheels remained up. Goldie Hanks rushed for the emergency let-down system and successfully got it working and the giant wheels fell into position.

One mile to go.

Gripping the wheel tightly, his seat and shoulder belts tightened for a possible crash landing, Captain Broocke gently lowered the DC-10 over the approach lights and eased her down the runway without a ripple, precisely nineteen minutes from the time of the explosion. As he brought the aircraft to a stop, the emergency equipment closed in. Smoke surrounded the aircraft, and passengers had to be evacuated as quickly as possible.

But still another problem arose. As the DC-10 came to a stop, stewardesses who were uninjured rushed to take their places at emergency exits, their first job to open the doors and deploy the emergency chutes. Six of the eight cabin exits were opened. The slide pack at the left forward door fell to the floor of the cabin instead of deploying outside the aircraft. A stewardess kicked it out the door. But it did not inflate and she began to read the instructions for the operation of the slides, something that she would not have time to do in case of a fire-followed accident. But she could not see the "red handle" which was to be pulled to start the slide inflation. It was located in such a position that it could not be "immediately visible" to the stewardess.

The emergency slide at the right forward door fell down and out as it was supposed to, but it, too, did not inflate. However, it was subsequently inflated after emergency measures were adopted. The escape slide at the right side over the wing did not deploy across the engine pylon as it was designed to do. It lay like an expired snake across the wing and was therefore useless.

Passengers lost little time in scrambling to safety. Many of them held back to assist the injured to safety. In the case of fire, passengers rarely help others. They cannot be blamed for such decisions.

Twenty-four persons were carried in a fleet of ambulances to Kirtland Air Force Base. Only then did the crew learn to their horror that passenger Gardner had been sucked out the open window to his death. Not even the stewardesses on duty in the cabin had known.

The New Mexico State Police and local organizations searched extensively for the missing machinist, but even with the assistance of computer analysis, which narrowed the search pattern by projecting the trajectories of a falling body from such a height, Gardner was never found.

9

The Autopsy of an Airliner

The National Transportation Safety Board was notified of the accident at five o'clock, only minutes after National Flight 27 was safely on the ground. It moved quickly to investigate.

Following the pattern set for the probing of other crashes, the Board established working groups for operations: Air Traffic Control, power plants, structures, systems, human factors, maintenance records, automatic flight systems, digital flight data recorder, and cockpit voice recorder.

Other parties requested to assist in the investigation included National Airlines, the Federal Aviation Administration, McDonnell-Douglas Aircraft Corporation, General Electric, the Air Line Pilots Association, and the Flight Engineers International Association. Augmenting this investigative group was a series of public hearings held in Miami for a total of six days during December 1973 and February 1974.

It was not until January 15, 1975, that the full report of the Safety Board's findings and recommendations was distributed. This was almost fifteen months after the accident, an indication of the length of time required to discover and evaluate the problems of Flight 27 and to recommend to the FAA the multiple changes required to ensure passenger safety.

The chain reaction of failures began within the number-three engine, located on the right wing. This was initiated by the experiments in the cockpit which caused the engine to run faster than its design strength allowed, and the tips of the fan blades began to vibrate. The space between the fan tips and the surrounding shroud is so narrow that when the vibration started, the tips began to rub against the shroud, setting up frictional forces that caused them to fly apart.

The huge fan located at the intake of each jet engine and clearly visible to an observer is not unlike a massive electric exhaust fan, which in a much smaller size in a familiar gadget in many modern kitchens. The aircraft jet fan draws tremendous amounts of air rearward into a series of compressors, which in turn squeeze the onrushing air into the burning chambers, where it is heated to fantastically high temperatures and is exhausted through turbine blades and finally expelled through massive pipes. It is the rush of rapidly expanding superheated air that creates the tremendous roar of a jet engine.

The intake fan supplies more than 70 per cent of the power of the aircraft. During the takeoff the fan is speeded up to the peak of its efficiency to provide the maximum intake and thrust of air to create the momentum that is necessary to increase air flow over the wings to provide the phenomenon of lift. As the airliner begins to gain speed and height, the speed of the fan and the other revolving parts of the engine is reduced through a throttle that commands the flow of fuel to the burners. Once the aircraft reaches its cruising altitude, the work of the fan is reduced because of the increased flow of air into the system created by the speed of the aircraft. This increased air flow is known as ram air. In the next century, airplanes will receive occasional bursts of speed from rockets, and the ram air thus generated will flow into burners and exhaust through a narrow pipe, a sophisticated system not unlike a child's balloon, which when filled with air will exhaust through a narrow opening and send the balloon scurrying in all directions. When the direction is controlled by a wing and a rudder, basic ram flight is achieved.

In the case of Flight 27, the fan tips broke away at the speed of a bullet, smashed through the Duralumin skin of the fuselage, severing the power controls en route and exiting through the other side of the cabin to rip into the engine on the far side.

Airlines and aircraft manufacturers are not responsible for design and operation of jet engines, but the maintenance, inspection, and periodic overhauling of the engines are the responsibility of the airlines. Most of the fan jet engines that power great Jumbo fleets are manufactured by General Electric, Pratt & Whitney, and Rolls-Royce. Until the introduction of the massive fan jets for Jumbos, the engines have churned along with superb performance and diminishing maintenance cost and inspections.

The engines that powered the DC-10 were built by General Electric. In checking back through maintenance log books of National Airlines, Safety Board investigators discovered to their amazement that between August 8 and September 12, 1973, there had been fifteen reports of problems with the particular engine which flew apart on Flight 27. On September 13, therefore, National's maintenance staff removed that engine for "major repairs." Ten days later it was replaced on the right wing of the DC-10 and between the time of replacement and the accident on November 3, some twenty-six faults involving that engine had been reported by pilots flying the aircraft.

Digging into other maintenance logs of airlines using the General Electric CF6-6 engine, investigators found similar fan failures. As far back as November 15, 1972, American Airlines removed a DC-10 engine after pilot reports of in-flight vibration, and while this engine was being tested at 3,308 revolutions per minute, slightly higher than normal flying speed, the whole engine blew apart.

This failure was investigated by American Airlines, Douglas Aircraft, and General Electric. It was found that five out of eleven attachment bolts failed with metal fatigue. This caused thirty-eight blades to leave the high-spinning rotor.

The second test-cell failure occurred on January 12, 1973, during a General Electric engineering investigation into the cause of fan blade vibration, which had been discovered in a production run. Special vibration instrumentation, a high-speed movie camera, a television camera, sound-recording equipment, and strobe lighting equipment were strategically placed to study the misbehaving fan.

Failure occurred during an attempted acceleration of the engine at 3,742 revolutions. The failure was caused by friction between the fan rotor and its casing. This caused the tips of the fan to rub against their shroud and as a number of fan blades left their disc, an imbalance was created and the whole thing flew apart—precisely what had happened to National's Flight 27 engine.

When it exploded, thirty-eight of the fan blades flew out of their slots. Although the Board found that the probable cause of the accident was an "interaction between the fan blade tips and the casing," caused by the acceleration of the engine, the precise reasons for the acceleration and the onset of the destructive vibration could not be determined conclusively.

As a result of this accident, the Safety Board made nine recommendations to the FAA. Three pertained to the inspection and maintenance of digital flight recorders. Five concerned the safety of passengers in relation to the oxygen systems installed in the DC-10, and one involved the assessment and report of aircraft damage by flight crews during emergencies. The latter was occasioned by the failure of stewardesses to tell the pilot of the visible damage that had occurred in the passenger compartments.

"Regardless of the cause of the high fan speed at the time of the fan failure, the Safety Board is concerned that the flight crew was, in effect, performing an untested failure analysis of the system. This type of experimentation, without benefit of training or specific guidelines, should never be performed during passenger flight operations," said the report.

The Board discovered that power could have been restored in certain areas by procedures outlined in the emergency check but that the engineer did not complete these check-list items.

On February 7, 1974, the Safety Board sent the following communication to the FAA:

Honorable Alexander P. Butterfield,
Administrator,
Federal Aviation Administration
Washington, D.C. 20591

The National Transportation Safety Board's continuing investigation of the National Airlines DC-10 accident near Albuquerque, New Mexico, on November 3, 1973, has disclosed unsafe conditions in the passenger oxygen system, portable oxygen system, and cabin pressurization system. The Board believes that these unsafe conditions merit your immediate attention and the attentions of all air carriers which operate aircraft with this equipment.

When the aircraft lost a cabin window and the passenger cabin decompressed, many of the passengers' oxygen-generating units were activated. Three oxygen canisters came out of their mountings in the seatback oxygen compartments and fell onto passenger seat cushions. Two of these canisters, which became very hot when operating, scorched the cushions and burned fingers when seat occupants tried to remove them.

The third reportedly caused a small fire. The canisters came out of their mounting brackets because of the pulling force exerted on either the initiation lanyard of the canisters or the oxygen supply hose. The Safety Board believes that these canisters constitute a potential fire and injury hazard when they are not retained properly in their mountings.

A subsequent inspection of a similar DC-10 aircraft at National Airlines' maintenance base in Miami, Florida, also revealed improperly mounted canisters. The improper mountings were a result of a slight distortion of the base plate and short mounting studs on the canister. Also, some of the oxygen supply hoses and the masks were improperly packaged. The Board found that shortcomings exist in both the design of the mounts of these oxygen units and related maintenance and servicing practices.

Another unsafe condition exists in the storage and availability of the portable oxygen equipment aboard the DC-10 aircraft. Portable oxygen bottles are contained in enclosed cabinets near the cabin attendants' stations. The regulator assemblies were covered with cellophane-type wrapping which was held by an elastic band. K-S disposable oxygen masks and supply tubing were sealed separately in plastic bags and stored with, or near, the portable oxygen bottles.

Paragraph (4) of 14 CFR 25.1447 "Equipment Standards for Oxygen Dispensing Units" requires that portable oxygen equipment be immediately available for each cabin attendant. The Board questions the "immediate availability" of such equipment when it must be unwrapped and assembled before it can be used, considering the reduced time of useful consciousness at flight level altitudes.

A *third* condition which the Board believes merits your attention is the distinct possibility that separate pressure losses of different magnitudes *may occur on the DC-10*. Preliminary estimates suggest that the lower lobe galley and the adjacent cargo compartment of the subject aircraft decompresses faster than the main passenger cabin or the cockpit area. This theory is reinforced by the fact that the two cabin attendants in the lower lobe galley lost consciousness almost immediately after the decompression.

The Board's concern about the third unsafe condition is twofold:

1. The aneroid device, which detects unacceptable cabin pressure altitudes in the aircraft and causes the oxygen dispensing units to be deployed automatically in such cases, is located in the ceiling of the forward passenger cabin. It controls the deployment of oxygen masks in the entire aircraft.

Therefore, if decompression occurred in the lower lobe of the aircraft, it might not be sensed by the aneroid device in the passenger cabin, and supplemental oxygen would not be available to the occupants in the lower galley. This apparently occurred in the subject accident, and both cabin attendants in this section of the aircraft lost consciousness as they attempted to retrieve the portable oxygen bottles. The Board believes that such a situation can seriously threaten the safety of occupants of the lower galley.

2. Two portable oxygen units which were located in the lower lobe galley of the aircraft were stowed on the forward wall of the galley and outboard of the escape ladder. One bottle was fitted with a "full-face" smoke mask, which was sealed in a plastic container. The other bottle was the type which must be fitted with a supply hose and a K-S disposable mask before it may be used. Not only is the Board concerned about the time

required to unpack parts for these units and assemble them, but it also believes that their location makes them virtually inaccessible when services carts are in their storage place in the galley.

Our staff has learned informally that some of the problems delineated above are being assessed by Flight Standards personnel of the FAA's Western Region to determine whether shortcomings in design and servicing exist.

The Safety Board is continuing its investigation and may make further recommendations regarding this accident. However, it believes that the safety of the traveling public requires immediate steps to prevent recurrence of the problems outlined above.

Accordingly, the National Transportation Safety Board recommends that the Federal Aviation Administration:

1. Require all operators of aircraft which contain individual chemical oxygen-generating units to inspect these installations to ensure that canisters are correctly installed in the mounts and that approved packing procedures have been followed for the supply hoses and oxygen masks.

2. Issue an Airworthiness Directive to require changes in the method of mounting these oxygen-generating units to eliminate the possibility of improper installation and in-service failure.

3. Issue a maintenance bulletin to verify operator compliance with the provision of 14 CFR 25.1447 regarding the immediate availability of portable oxygen units and the necessity of having supply hoses and masks attached to these units.

4. Issue an Airworthiness Directive to require aircraft certificated under 14 CFR 25, that each occupiable area, which is separated from others to such an extent that significantly different decompression rates can occur, is equipped with an aneroid device to detect pressure losses in that area.

5. Require a more accessible location for the portable oxygen units in the lower lobe galley of all DC-10 aircraft and relocate portable oxygen units in all other aircraft, where required, to ensure accessibility of portable oxygen units and compliance with the FAR's.

Personnel from our Bureau of Aviation Safety offices will be made available if any further information or assistance is desired.

REED, Chairman, McADAMS, and HALEY, Members, concurred in the above recommendations. THAYER and BURGESS, Members, were absent, not voting.

By: John H. Reed
Chairman

On February 21, 1974, the following letter was received in answer:

Honorable John H. Reed
Chairman, National Transportation Safety Board
Department of Transportation
Washington, D.C. 20591
Dear Mr. Chairman:
This is in response to NTSB Safety Recommendations A-74-7 thru -11.

Recommendation No. A-74-7. Require all operators of aircraft which contain individual chemical oxygen-generating units to inspect these installations to ensure that canisters are correctly installed in the mounts and that approved packing procedures have been followed for the supply hoses and oxygen masks.

Comment. We are issuing a maintenance bulletin which will instruct principal inspectors to review the air carrier operators' maintenance programs to determine that sufficient inspections are specified for the oxygen-generating units and associated supply hoses and masks. Principal inspectors will request more frequent inspections if necessary.

Recommendation No. A-74-8. Issue an Airworthiness Directive to require changes in the method of mounting these oxygen-generating units to eliminate the possibility of improper installation and in-service failures.

Comment. We are working with the Douglas Aircraft Company to assess the DC-10 passenger oxygen units. This investigation will result in a redesign and modification of the units. Airworthiness directives or other appropriate directives will be issued to implement the new design.

Recommendation No. A-74-9. Issue a maintenance bulletin to verify operator compliance with the provision of 14 CFR 25.1447 regarding the immediate availability of portable oxygen units and the necessity of having supply hoses and masks attached to these units.

Comment. The maintenance bulletin will include instructions to the principal inspectors to determine that portable oxygen bottles with hose and mask assemblies attached are immediately available to all crew members.

Recommendation No. A-74-10. Issue an Airworthiness Directive to require aircraft certificated under 14 CFR 25, that each occupiable area, which is separated from others to such an extent that significantly different decompression rates can occur, is equipped with an aneroid device to detect pressure losses in that area.

Comment. We are working with Douglas to determine the best method to prevent significant pressure differentials in different compartments from occurring and what changes in the aneroid system are required to ensure oxygen system operation in all areas.

Recommendation No. A-74-11. Require a more accessible location for the portable oxygen units in the lower lobe galley of all DC-10 aircraft and relocate portable oxygen units in all other aircraft, where required, to ensure accessibility of portable oxygen units and compliance with the FAR's.

Comment. We are working with Douglas to select more accessible locations for the portable oxygen units in the lower lobe galley. When the new locations are determined, we will take appropriate action to implement relocation.

Sincerely,

Alexander P. Butterfield
Administrator

But by the end of the year the FAA was severely criticized by the news and television media for its failure to take action on these DC-10 problems. During these attacks of unprecedented severity, the New York *Times* revealed on December 27, 1974, the existence of a report written during the previous April by a ten-man inquiry board headed by Oscar Bakke, then the associate administrator of the FAA. Bakke retired from his post in the summer of 1974 without seeing his report published.

The communication cited the FAA's actions in certifying the DC-10 as "questionable," and called its later corrective actions on the hatch door problem "ineffective." The board made eight recommendations, some of which were never acted upon.

A government report from a special subcommittee of the House of Representatives, issued at the same time as the newspaper attack, accused the FAA of: "Sluggishness which at times approaches an attitude of indifference to public safety . . . completely inappropriate bureaucratic slowness to act, and inaction which might literally endanger human life."

The day after this report was issued, the American Broadcasting Company released an hour-long documentary entitled *Crashes: The Illusion of Safety.*

The documentary, narrated by aerospace writer Jules Bergman, focused attention on the current air safety problems and on the FAA's failure to deal with them.

One of the items that ABC released was a memo from an engineer of the General Dynamics Company, the company that built the DC-10 cargo door system, to McDonnell-Douglas, on June 27, 1972. It read: "It seems to me inevitable that the DC-10 cargo doors will come open. I would expect this to usually result in the loss of the airplane."

Alexander Butterfield, FAA administrator and former White House aide, told Bergman that he had never seen the memo and was not aware if any of his staff had seen it. In the same interview, Butterfield promised there would be FAA action on visibility standards for emergency exit signs "in about three weeks" and on flammability standards for the uniforms of the flight attendants "soon."

Bergman told his audience that the interview had been taped six weeks earlier and no action had been taken since. The FAA had no comment.

But there was more to follow. On March 1, 1975, the FAA issued a "telegraphic alert" to all DC-10 operators that a problem existed with the main doors of the passenger cabins. This directive was triggered by an accident on an American Airlines flight, outbound from Los Angeles to Boston, on February 28, 1975. The rear right door blew inward at 1,200 feet. The FAA was previously aware that passenger door problems had cropped up with Northwest, Delta, and United Airlines.

The FAA gave all operators thirty days to conduct door inspections to determine if the cables on the doors had been misrigged. If they had been, they were to be immediately replaced. One official of American Airlines revealed that the situation had become so critical with the DC-10 that cabin attendants had been warned to keep passengers seated some distance from the doors until all repairs were completed.

The U.S. transport industry was in a quandary. In 1974, earnings had been a comfortable $375 million, up from $200 million in 1973. But safety deficiency was raising insurance costs and passenger apprehension.

On Monday, July 8, 1974, National Airlines reported that one of its DC-10s ran into trouble when the cowling came off the number-one engine, smashed back into the leading edge of the left wing, bounced over the top of it, and collided with the rear part of the passenger cabin before being sucked into the intake of number-two engine on the tail. Number-two engine disintegrated.

The DC-10 involved was the same plane that was involved in the Albuquerque incident on November 3, 1973.

There must have been many airlines at this juncture who wished they had never heard of the DC-10. Yet, unfortunate as it seems, the bugs that develop in new breeds of aircraft usually appear after the planes have been flown for thousands of hours after being certified as safe for flying.

It is one of the more frightening aspects of aviation. The safety gap is further narrowed appreciably when other factors involving pilots and environment are introduced.

PART III

The Sinister Envelope
of Air

10

Bad Weather—Lethal and Unpredictable

The aviation industry, concerned with design problems, constant and costly modification to aircraft to meet design changes, and government directives to reduce noise and pollution, was further shaken to learn that of the twenty-four airliner accidents in 1976, seven were caused by tubulent weather.

In each case the turbulence caused serious injuries to crews and passengers, but there were hundreds of other bad-weather encounters that caused severe shaking-ups and the passenger apprehension that accompanies such turbulence.

Some people in the industry were ready to blame the sheer massiveness of the Jumbos for the sharp rise in injuries resulting from these encounters. But the worst weather-caused crash in U.S. history involved not a Jumbo but a 727, the world's most popular airliner, which is an indication that severe turbulence does not seek out any particular aircraft. Light to moderate turbulence does, however, give passengers a rude shaking in Jumbos more than in the sleeker varieties of jets.

Blame for the bad-weather encounters was also directed at the weather forecasters, at poor flying techniques, and perhaps worst of all, at the insufficient training of flight crews to enable them to recognize and avoid troublesome weather phenomena.

It seems incredible in this modern age, with computerized forecasting and a vast worldwide network of weather communication, that airliners should fly into turbulence. Satellite reports are fed into ground-based computers every hour. Severe storms are predicted around the clock at the U. S. Weather Bureau Center at Kansas City. These are augmented by high- and low-altitude reports and the monitoring of high- and low-pressure systems from stations in every corner of the continent and from ships at sea and from foreign stations.

Why do pilots take off in bad weather when the prudent course would be to remain on the ground until conditions improve? Why do they fly into storms instead of asking to be rerouted around them? Why do they land at airports when snow, sleet, hail, and tornadic winds make it unsafe to do so? There are several reasons; one of them is that airlines like to keep their passengers happy by keeping to their schedules. Litigation may soon change this attitude since common sense does not seem to prevail.

An example of the kind of problem a flight crew faces in bad weather occurred on the stormy afternoon of December 17, 1973. Iberia Airlines Flight 933 had almost completed a delightful voyage across the Atlantic and was making its final approach into Boston. Low scud clouds laced with black and ominous showers churned capriciously over the ocean shoreline. The clouds swirled and eddied along the flight path, creating turbulence and diminishing visibility on the ground.

Although Boston's Logan Airport has always been regarded by pilots as a good airport, having few obstacles on the final approach from the sea, it is, like many airports in the world, severely deficient in meteorological information. It had no equipment for measuring winds aloft; nor were there updated weather reports or warnings from other pilots regarding the adverse wind conditions that were flowing into the final approach path that afternoon.

The nasty storm at Boston had not been predicted by weather forecasters at Madrid when Captain Jesus Caleron Gaztelu and his fellow flight officers, co-pilot Alfredo Perez Vega and engineer Celodonio Martin Santes were briefed before their ocean hop. But transatlantic crews are familiar with the weather changes that can occur during a seven-hour flight, and the Iberia crew was not surprised to learn on approaching the U.S. seacoast that airport visibility was down to 300 feet with rain and fog cutting visibility to three quarters of a mile.

Captain Gaztelu started down through the clouds, using the automatic pilot of the DC-10 to place him on the electronic glide slope to the active runway, 33-Left. The tower reported to him that a moderate 9-knot wind was blowing from the northwest, which would place it about 43 degrees off the line of the invisible runway. The temperature was 41° F. at ground level, which would indicate to experienced pilots like Gaztelu that icing conditions at low altitudes could be expected.

After making the preliminary landing checks, the on-board computer flashed the digital message that in order to overcome the possibility of unexpected wind gusting, the DC-10 should touch the threshold of the runway at 140 knots, about 15 knots faster than the speed for normal fine-weather landings.

The airliner descended and turned, placed by the pilot in perfect alignment and speed for the coming landing. The tower informed the flight that the runway was wet and slippery. The crew was therefore aware that the braking action of wheel brakes and reverse thrust of the engines would be below average, but such conditions were familiar and not considered hazardous.

Descending through the fog and rain, they experienced some turbulence, as expected, but the DC-10 maintained its rigid stability for the landing a few seconds away. The flashing approach lights to the runway appeared through the haze, a welcome sight to crew and passengers alike.

"Slightly to our left," the first officer reported to his captain, in referring to the line-up of beckoning lights. Captain Gaztelu flipped the button on his wheel that disconnected the autopilot and grasped the yoke tightly to land the aircraft manually. "Runway in sight," the first officer reported.

The captain and first officer of an Air Canada DC-9, which was parked on the taxiway adjacent to 33-Left, saw the Iberia flight emerge from the fog less than a mile to the east of their position.

"Desperately low," observed the Air Canada captain.

"Too low to recover," replied the first officer.

Back on the DC-10, engineer Santes was following the book by calling out the approach altitudes: "Fifty feet . . . forty . . . thirty . . . twenty . . . ten . . ."

The flight crew was unaware that Boston's radio glidepath, which they were dutifully following on their instrument panel, had not been corrected to comply with FAA directional changes issued on February 24, 1972, establishing standards of wheel clearance for Jumbo jets. The sensing device in the nose of the airliner receiving its information from a transmitter at the threshold to line the plane along the glidepath for the touchdown had not been adjusted to provide more height for Jumbos so that the wheels would clear the approach lights. But this had no bearing on the events of the next few seconds.

The airliner wavered, then sank suddenly with a stomach-churning feeling of an elevator that was free-falling. There were screams in the passenger compartments, shouts on the flight deck. The DC-10 struck an approach light on a pier just off the shoreline and close to the threshold.

It continued on. Stricken because of the loss of inertial speed, it smashed its way through all the approach lights in its path like a monster consuming frail vegetation. Then it struck an embankment and the force of the collision slammed the captain's seat so far back he could no longer see the airport. But he pushed forward on the control column anyway, to force an immediate contact with the ground. The plane hit the runway and the landing gear collapsed in an unrecognizable mess of wheels, tires, belly fuselage, and support structures.

The DC-10 bounced into the air, fell back on the runway, and skidded to a stop in the grass to the right of the concrete. Fire erupted from the left wing as spilled fuel flowed over the sparks caused by frictional contact with the concrete.

The crew had the presence of mind to radio the tower: "We have an accident."

Rushing to the glass window and peering into the fog, the controller saw a trail of fire along the runway and pulled the fire alarm. Incredibly, none of the 167 persons aboard the aircraft perished in the explosion and fire that followed. But luck and luck alone was the savior. Stewardesses reported they could open neither the main right forward door nor the left rear door.

Although the DC-10 has eight escape exits, four on each side, passengers had to scramble through the only two available for escape. Flames mushrooming over the left side had effectively cut off the others as well as the right forward door and two mid-doors. One crew member and fifteen passengers were injured when they jumped to the ground. Five persons were trapped in the aft part of the fuselage because the aisles were blocked when the rear floor was forced up three feet in a tangle of seats and partitions.

Four of those trapped managed to escape by squeezing through a crack in the side of the aircraft. The fifth was pulled from the tangle by an alert stewardess. Grouped together afterward, the distraught passengers declared their lives had been saved by a miracle. Someone remembered that the captain's name was Jesus.

After word of this near-tragedy flashed to Washington, the largest investigation force in the history of the Safety Board descended on Boston. When a $24 million airplane flies into the ground, a lot of people want to know why. The fact that it was a DC-10 gave added impetus to the various teams assigned to study the human factors, weather, and aircraft behavior involved in the case.

Painstaking investigation of the working parts of the expired DC-10 showed that all systems and controls appeared to be working properly at the time of the mishap. The flight recorder, retrieved from the tailpiece in perfect condition, confirmed these findings.

The flight recorder also provided the clue to the mystery. It revealed that the airliner was descending normally at 840 feet a minute and at an altitude of 400 feet the automatic pilot was shut down and the captain took over the controls. But a few seconds later the altitude had decreased to 200 feet and the descent rate of the altimeter recorded on tape revealed that the Jumbo was descending straight down at a rate of 1,170 feet a minute.

This was as though the aircraft had lost all its power and was falling like a stone. The phenomenon lacked explanation for the moment but the Safety Board turned to the weather, aware of the violence and caprices of churning winds and turbulence. Then, armed with all the available data from weather instruments located in a 60-mile circle of Boston, the Safety Board fed all the pertinent information into a computer to establish the precise landing conditions of the Iberia flight and then asked for five volunteers from a list of captains of other airlines to fly a simulated flight.

Each pilot discovered while flying the simulator of the DC-10 that was programmed to the wind changes that, when switching from automatic pilot to manual control as Captain Gaztelu had done, the descent rate increased alarmingly and the only way he could avoid a "crash" was to pull the angle of the plane upward and accomplish this in six seconds.

Even when the five pilots anticipated the sudden wind changes during those last seconds of final approach, the DC-10 was ten feet or less above the approach lights, a distance that left no margin whatsoever for safety. The tests showed that pilots would have to change the angle and speed of the Jumbo in four seconds to save the approach, a frightening indication of the slim safety margin of landing a modern, wide-bodied jet in turbulent weather.

Weather. The Safety Board was convinced that atmospheric violence was the culprit. By studying charts and weather instrument recordings, the Board found that the Iberia flight had encountered a 29-knot tail wind while descending through the 500-foot level. This would have provided a considerable forward shove when added to the speed of the aircraft. Then, at 200-foot altitude, the jet had run into a reverse wind of 5 knots on the nose. When winds flow in opposite directions, the dividing line between them is known as wind shear.

Wind shear would soon be a term to remember. It is familiar to pilots flying through thunderstorms where the line of updrafts and downdrafts can be expected. It causes the ups and downs that an airliner experiences in flying through storms and, as all passengers know, it is extremely uncomfortable. Some wind shears are created by countermoving drafts of such velocity that any aircraft, particularly the thin-winged jets, can be tossed out of control. Hence, that is the reason thunderstorms should be avoided.

Wind shear immediately above the ground is difficult to predict with any accuracy and it strikes an airliner just at the critical moment of final approach, when the angle of the aircraft and the speed are mathematically established to effect perfect descent to the concrete.

The Iberia crew got caught in the unpredictable swirl of winds and are lucky to be still flying.

11

Wind Shear

The phenomenon of wind shear has been associated with the storms of the lower atmosphere since the dawn of time but was unimportant until the age of flight. Propeller aircraft were never disturbed by wind shear because of the quick response of the propeller to move large volumes of air and increase speed in a few seconds. Jets require some six to ten seconds to respond to the movement of the throttles and in that brief time changes of the wind play havoc with their speed. Having become aware of this fact because of catastrophes and near-disasters, the Air Lines Pilots Association has issued many warnings to pilots to be on the lookout for this hazard during their final landing approaches under storm conditions.

Unfortunately these warnings haven't done much good.

The All-Weather Flying Committee, headed by Captain J. L. DeCelles and Captain E. J. Burke of American Airlines, investigating the effects of bad weather surrounding airports, discovered many instances of final approach problems during rapid wind changes. This information has been provided to all its thirty thousand member pilots, to the members of the Canadian Air Line Pilots Association, and to all safety organizations including the FAA and the Safety Board.

One incident investigated by ALPA was the descent of an airliner toward a short hilltop runway. (The date, the name of the airport, and the operator were not revealed.) The crew saw the approach lights and continued their descent toward them. But six seconds later there was a sudden shift in the wind. The pilot became alarmed and started to pull up, but almost immediately the plane slammed into the trees a mile short of the runway. There were no survivors.

There was also the crash of a flight approaching an airport at night over water while the automatic pilot was engaged and locked into the instrument landing system. A strong tail wind during the first phase of the descent veered to a head wind, which slackened in velocity as the airliner continued to descend. In a situation almost identical to the Iberia incident, the crew of this flight reported to the tower: "Approach lights in sight."

But wind shear was ominously lurking along the line of approach. The airliner had dipped 50 feet below the glide path because of the decrease in the head wind. The nose of the plane pitched up as the auto-pilot attempted to maintain its electronic position on the glide slope.

The captain and his co-pilot were aware of the change because the runway lights had changed position in their windshield. From years of flying, pilots can tell if they are on the right slope to the lights by the position of the lights in their windshield. In fact, some aircraft have lines in the windshield to show where such lights should be if the plane is on the right glide path.

It was estimated that it took the crew about five seconds to realize the lights were in the wrong place. The jet struck the approach lights at a height of 50 feet above the ground. The main landing gear was torn away and the airliner continued onto the runway with a heavy bounce. Fortunately no injuries or deaths resulted from this mishap. On another occasion, ALPA reported that a cargo jet was 2 miles from touchdown when it collided with a wind shear. It dived into the ground from loss of control and the crew was killed and the aircraft and cargo destroyed.

Wind shear is not associated only with fog and rain and

swirling clouds. It can occur when visibility is reasonably good, as happened at Kennedy Airport on June 24, 1975.

Black cumulus clouds boiled over New York City, darkening the sky up to 40,000 feet. Lightning bolts arced through the clouds and crashed earthward with fiery pyrotechnics. Yet visibility was 2 miles and the ceiling was 5,000 feet. Airliners dropping through cloud cover over Jamaica Bay could see Kennedy clearly.

During the early afternoon the weather radar at Kennedy and at the Air Traffic Control Center at nearby Islip, Long Island, picked up echoes of hooked formations in the nearby storm clouds. Hooked clouds or swirls in the leading edges of thunderstorms always indicate the presence of severe turbulence, hail, and sometimes tornadoes. These appear on radar as a figure eight.

These conditions did not deter the landings and takeoffs of the great jet fleet at Kennedy. Storms do not stop such traffic. Passenger fears are minimized when bolts of lightning bounce off the wet surfaces of the airliners because captains report over the intercom system: "There is nothing to fear, ladies and gentlemen. Lightning cannot harm us and there is no case of lightning ever harming an airliner."

At 3:56 P.M. that day a Flying Tiger DC-8 cargo jet approached Runway 22-Left. Suddenly a swirl of cloud-filled winds enveloped the 350,000-pound plane and shook it like a dog worrying a rabbit. Pilot Jack Bliss fought to retain control and called the Kennedy tower: "Wind shear on approach . . . The wind pulls you down and turns you over . . . You should close the runway." He landed safely a few minutes after this alert.

Two minutes later an Eastern Airlines Lockheed 1011 Jumbo, operating as Flight 902, descended toward the runway and became caught in the same turbulence. The aircraft pitched violently and pilot Clifton Nickerson alerted the tower: "Wind shear and turbulence." Having given the warning, Nickerson fought to keep his giant aircraft on an even keel and in order to save it, pulled up, poured on more power, and swung over to Newark Airport, where a safe landing was made.

From past experience, he knew that Jumbos are vulnerable to severe turbulence because of their massive size—like a circus tent in a windstorm.

The runway was not closed by Approach Control, even after these two warnings. Then at four o'clock, two minutes after the Eastern alert, a Finnair DC-8 arriving after the long hop from Helsinki touched down without any problem on Runway 22-Left. Three minutes later a Beechcraft Baron landed on the same strip without difficulty.

At 4:06 P.M., a scant three minutes after the uneventful landing of the Beechcraft, Eastern's Flight 66 from New Orleans was on its final approach to Kennedy. Captain John W. Kleven, fifty-four, had been advised minutes before by the tower that Eastern's Flight 902 had complained of wind shear.

Easing his stretched 727 over the marshland that separates Kennedy from the beaches along the ocean, Kleven held tightly to the wheel of the sleek white airliner as it roared toward the runway. Still some 2,300 feet from the edge of the runway, the flight struck a row of 22-foot-high towers that support runway approach lights.

The jet was 100 feet below the glide slope when it struck pylons 7, 8, and 9 in succession. The aircraft pulled up slightly and then demolished pylons 13 through 17, slewed to the left into the sodden ground, and immediately caught fire.

As the plane was ripped apart, a 45-foot slice of fuselage spun across the swampy field, broke through a stout wire fence, and caromed across Rockaway Boulevard, which an hour later would have been solidly jammed with homeward-bound traffic. The rear section came to rest upside down in the field, a mass of flames.

Amazingly, a stewardess, Mary Mooney, twenty-eight, of Tulsa, Oklahoma, and a steward, Robert Hoefler, twenty-nine, of New York, managed to tumble out of the wreckage in a dazed condition. They had been seated in the last row of seats. Twelve passengers were found alive by rescuers. The remaining 110 were reduced to broken bodies. One of the survivors died later from injuries.

There were twenty-seven witnesses to the crash and many of

them said they saw the plane struck by lightning just before it plunged to the ground. But the Safety Board investigators, though not discrediting reports of lightning, found the culprit to be the reported wind shear.

Questioned by reporters as to why he had no trouble in landing that day, the Finnair DC-8 pilot said that his aircraft was equipped with an Inertial Navigation System (INS), which enabled him to monitor wind velocity and duration. He was therefore aware of possible wind shear and he had set his approach speed accordingly.

The Eastern flights were not equipped with this navigational system. In fact, very few airlines and only a handful of aircraft have it. The main reason is the cost, about $200,000 for each machine.

Air Canada, Trans World Airlines, and Pan Am have had INS in their 747 planes for the past five years. Air Canada also has the system in their DC-8 stretched jets, but not in the Lockheed 1011s, because the navigational system installed by Lockheed is one of the finest packages in service today.

The INS consists of two independent units that display on instrument panels the ground speed and the sideways drift of the aircraft. These dials are monitored not only by the first officer but also by the second officer in planes such as the Jumbo 747. The system is not coupled to the automatic pilot, even when it is locked into the Instrument Landing Approach System. Therefore, when the presence of wind shear appears on the dials, it is relayed by word of mouth every second of the landing sequence, and if shear is spotted, instant action is taken by the captain in command to increase the power to the engines.

Air Canada pilots, familiar with the system and finding it exclusive on many of their flights with scores of other aircraft around them, will alert the tower of the presence and severity of wind shear. Other airline pilots have been known to do the same if they have INS aboard.

At the time of the Eastern disaster there was no known ground system to predict wind shear in the periphery of airports despite the fact that the phenomenon is a natural participant in the movement of thunderstorms as well as the intrusion of cold fronts into the vicinity of warm ocean air along seacoasts.

Although the Eastern crash occurred in June 1975, it was not until early 1976 that a wind-shear detection effort was pushed by the FAA. Bureaucracy is no excuse for such tardiness. It was announced that a number of government agencies had been contacted to develop, if possible, a ground and air technique for predicting and detecting the hazard. Involved were the National Oceanic and Atmospheric Administration, the Defense Department, the National Aeronautics and Space Administration, the National Transportation Safety Board, and the Transportation Systems Center. The FAA also contacted the airlines and industrial contractors.

The FAA said that investigation of the phenomenon indicated that wind-shear conditions are generated by a temperature inversion during the passage of a weather front or a thunderstorm. A weather front covers a large area and is more easily detectable because its movement can be measured more accurately. Thunderstorms, however, are localized phenomena and it is much more difficult to determine when wind shears are associated with them. The Safety Board revealed that most of the air accidents are associated with thunderstorms. A survey showed that more than one in every five accidents involved turbulence and one in every sixteen encounters produced fatalities.

Soon after the announcement of the all-out fight to predict wind shear, the FAA announced that more than a dozen airborne devices were suggested and McDonnell-Douglas was asked to give each of them an evaluation on a DC-10 simulator. These tests are going on at the present time.

The FAA learned, meanwhile, that the use of inexpensive ground sensors around the perimeter of airports could detect the presence, severity, and direction of wind shear. These sensors are designed to detect a rapid change in barometric pressure over a period of one minute. They are called "pressure-jump" sensors and were developed by the National Oceanic and Atmospheric Administration's Wave Propagation Laboratory in Boulder, Colorado.

Pressure-jump sensors, each mounted on a telephone pole about three quarters of a mile apart, are now under operational tests at Chicago's O'Hare, Washington's Dulles, and an unnamed air force base. At East Coast airports experiments are being conducted with a technique developed by Northwest Airlines to predict wind shear caused by frontal movements, when masses of warm or cold air are moving across the land to bring changes in the weather.

Also installed at Dulles Airport is a Doppler radar to detect wind shear from any cause. This narrow-beam vertical-looking acoustic radar is expected to measure both wind speed and its direction. Unfortunately, acoustic radar does not function well in adverse weather and under rain conditions, so the FAA plans to back up the Doppler system with a microwave radar to provide all-weather capability.

"We know very little about wind shear," admitted Fred Coons, the FAA's meteorologist assigned to the wind-shear effort. "The data so far collected is so gross that it cannot identify many of the characteristics of wind shear when it does occur. Frequently we discover we had wind-shear conditions after the fact—from pilots or subsequent examination of weather conditions at the airport."

If and when the phenomenon can be positively detected, the FAA has another phenomenon to work on. It is called anti-gravitational wave.

12

A Hand Reached Out
from the Sky

On the hazy afternoon of November 16, 1969, an atmospheric phenomenon startled weather bureaus across the United States and created a serious rift between the FAA and the Air Lines Pilots Association. It also paralyzed a competent air crew and a large number of passengers with an awesome and unexpected display of the forces of nature.

The weather that day over southern Michigan was changing rapidly, but this was not uncommon for that time of year. Lazy breezes over Lake Erie blended into the industrial dust of Detroit's mighty array of smoke-producing steel mills and iron foundries to create a familiar copper-toned umbrella over the countryside. It was warm and slightly humid due to a moisture-filled low-pressure system that was centered over Illinois and traveling leisurely in a northeasterly direction.

Moving rapidly toward this balmy and unstable air mass was a high-pressure system of frigid air from northern Canada. Weathermen know that the meeting of hot and cold air masses creates all the weather patterns of the United States and Canada, and the speed at which they clash determines the difference between mild and stormy weather.

Watching the movement of the pressure systems by long-distance radar and combining this information with radio reports from high-altitude balloons and barometric stations dotted across the continent, the Severe Storm Warning Center at Kansas City issued a bulletin that tornadoes could be expected over southern Michigan between four and seven o'clock that day.

Captain William Hunt of United Airlines learned of the severe storm warning at the usual pre-flight briefing at Detroit Metropolitan Airport. He noted with satisfaction that his intended route to Milwaukee would be clear sailing.

While walking to his Boeing 727 parked at the western end of the huge terminal, Captain Hunt chatted with the ramp agent. His co-pilot walked around the aircraft to make his regular visual inspection of the flying surfaces and to check the tires of the landing gear for low pressure or damage.

"What's our loading today?"

"Very light, Captain, about forty, maybe fifty passengers," answered the ramp agent.

"All the more steak for me," Hunt laughed as he boarded the airliner by the front left-side steps. (The Boeing 727 also has a loading ramp in the rear, under the tailpiece.)

Captain Hunt waved a greeting to the pretty cabin attendants and took his place on the flight deck, in the traditional left-hand seat. He was joined by his co-pilot while his engineer was activating the power instruments on the panel on the right side of the flight deck, immediately behind the co-pilot's seat. Glowing lights snapped to attention as the engineer checked the pumping and electrical systems of the three-engine aircraft.

It was 4:30 P.M.

The shaking of the airliner meant that passengers were boarding. Captain Hunt talked with Detroit Ground Control, advising that he was turning on the engines. The engineer pushed the starter buttons, first for number-one engine on the left wing, watching the revolutions of the engine until it had reached the speed when the fuel would take over from the starter. At that second he opened the fuel cock by pushing a fuel lever to full open. Next he brought to life the engine on the tail and lastly, the third engine on the right wing.

"All okay," he said.

The instrument check-off completed, Captain Hunt moved

the airliner to the active runway area and switched his radio frequency to Detroit Departure Control.

"Any delay?" asked Captain Hunt.

"Okay, after American lands . . . There's a Northeast seven miles behind."

"Roger, after American."

Captain Hunt watched the American Airlines 707 flare out for the landing and then touch the runway in front of him and roar along the concrete in a cloud of smoke as the reverse thrust of its four engines overcame the forward speed. As American cleared the active runway, Captain Hunt was already in place for the rapid takeoff. Shoving the three throttles forward, he brought the 727 to full life and in twenty-six seconds it divorced itself from the runway.

The aircraft turned left over the busy Ford Expressway as the thump of the wheels being tucked in activated a light on the control panels that all was in order. In ten seconds the dim outline of Willow Run Airport below the aircraft was spotted for a second or two before the flight was closed in by haze.

Still under Detroit Departure Control, the co-pilot informed the center that United was "at four thousand and climbing."

The soft sigh of the wing flaps being drawn into the trailing edges of the wings and the reduction of power for the climb to cruising height gave promise of an uneventful flight ahead.

Then it happened. Without the slightest warning, the 60-ton airliner began to rise vertically into the sky. Three altimeters confirmed that the 727 was rising straight up at an extremely high rate of speed. There was no forward motion whatsoever.

There was consternation in the cockpit. At first the crew thought that something had gone wrong with the instruments. They were registering a vertical ascent of such magnitude that the flight had risen from 5,000 to 8,000 feet in one second. Incredible! And it was still rising.

Every person on board was being squeezed into his seat by tremendous G-forces. Seat belts, tight a moment before, were now flapping loosely as bodies were forced back into the limits of the foam cushions. It felt as if a giant hand had grabbed hold of the airliner and was lifting it straight up.

Captain Hunt and his fellow officers saw the the speed instruments were down to zero, as they would be if the aircraft were on the ground.

"Something's gone wrong with United!" yelled the departure controller, who was just getting ready to turn the flight over to Air Route Traffic Control. Other controllers in the dimly lit center rushed to the departure scope. They could see the blip of light that marked United but could not see any trail that should have been visible behind the flight indicating outward motion from the airport area. Calls to the aircraft brought no response. Some of the controllers thought that something had gone wrong with their radar except that other departing flights were visible and the blips were behaving in a normal manner.

And the 727 was still going up . . . up . . . up.

Captain Hunt had been told time and again that when an airliner is caught in convection currents it is not permissible to alter the attitude of the jet by trimming it up or down. Fledgling pilots learn that trimming is required to provide the aircraft with the best attitude for flight, which in reality simply means the smoothest slope for penetrating the air stream. This is accomplished in all aircraft by a trim wheel in the cockpit which activates an aerodynamic empennage on the tail of the aircraft to make slight changes in the wind direction which will then lower or raise the nose of the aircraft.

If the trim wheel in the cockpit is moved forward, the nose of the aircraft in flight will dip down several degrees. If the wheel is moved rearward or clockwise, the nose will rise a few degrees. It is necessary to place the aircraft in a nose-up position for takeoff and landing in order to receive the full benefit of lift from the wings when the speed of the air flowing over the wings has been slowed down. As the aircraft gathers speed, the loss of flow over the wings is compensated for and the aircraft is usually trimmed to an even position. In propeller-driven aircraft a gust of wind raises the nose up slightly and the pilot uses his trim wheel to lower the nose to keep the aircraft on an even keel. If a downdraft should send the nose down slightly the aircraft can be trimmed upward to maintain an even attitude. This practice is routine in all propeller aircraft.

Jet airliners, however, are particularly sensitive to trimming because of their high speed and their aerodynamic shape with thin rearward-angled wings. They are prone to stall either at high speed or low speed if the combination of wind speed and aerodynamics is disturbed—and trimming can disturb this combination.

Raising the nose of an airliner can slow it down. Lowering the nose can speed it up. It took the loss of many lives to demonstrate that you don't trim a jet to achieve attitude balance more than perhaps a degree or two, if that. The reason is not complex. If the nose of the jet is forced upward by a convection current, for instance, and the pilot trims the nose downward to maintain the level attitude and a split second later a downdraft shoves the nose down, the aircraft, already trimmed down, goes into a dive, which most often is unrecoverable because of the fantastic speed that quickly develops, usually above the speed of sound. Jet pilots learned to their dismay, after a number of fatal crashes and flight tests by the FAA, that it often takes some 20,000 feet of altitude to bring a plunging jet under control.

Finding the nose of his airliner going up, Captain Hunt, despite what he had been told, trimmed the nose downward. The aircraft continued to ascend.

Up, up . . . 9,000 feet . . . 10,000 . . .

The flight crew could not hear the screams of fear from the passenger cabin, nor the moans of the bewildered, nor the mumbling of prayers.

Suddenly the aircraft broke through the thick stratus cloud into clear sky. It hesitated. For a split unreal second it was motionless in the air. Then, under the power of the engines which until that moment had been churning to no avail, and with the aircraft trimmed to a nose-down position, the 727 dived back into the cloud and headed almost straight down toward the ground—2 miles below.

Captain Hunt, with both his co-pilot and engineer lending a hand, pulled back on the yoke to try and get the aircraft into level flight. Responding to this slight change in its control surfaces, the plane began to roller-coaster like a crazy thing.

"God save us," shouted a passenger.

Stewardesses were tossed into the ceiling and were just as quickly hurled back to the floor.

"We're going in . . . going in . . ." shouted Captain Hunt into his microphone, still in contact with Departure Control.

"Good Christ, what's happening?" gasped the controller as other mystified controllers stood over the glow of the radar scope.

"United's in real trouble," one of them murmured.

Back on the United flight, an infant, dragged from its mother's arms by the girations of the aircraft and then caught in the weightlessness of roller-coastering, floated over the aisle a few feet above the floor.

"Just like an angel floating by," commented one of the passengers. A woman, not the mother, grabbed the baby and clutched it to her breast.

A youth, his belt secured, was sucked out of the belt to the ceiling and the belt caught around his ankles. As suddenly as he went up, he came down and landed with a resounding thud in his seat. One woman, her belt secured, was thrown to the aisle and spun around like a whirling top. The contents of stomachs spewed onto the floor and into laps.

At the last moment Captain Hunt's superhuman efforts were able to bring the 727 into level flight. When he dared to look out the window he was startled to see a farmhouse and then a barn slip rearward under his wings.

His altimeter read 240 feet above the ground.

The FAA, never willing to ground an airliner, grounded Captain Hunt instead. His license was revoked because he had trimmed his aircraft to a nose-down degree that was not permissible by the flight standards of United Airlines. This meant that Captain Hunt was finished as a commercial pilot unless he could prove that his action had been justified. With the assistance of the Air Lines Pilots Association, he appealed to the Civil Aeronautics Board and after a long and involved investigation, the Board found that Captain Hunt was trying to save his flight under circumstances that had never before been experienced, and for that reason his transport license was returned to him.

The Safety Board, never interested in the turbulence that jets encounter somewhere every day of the week, had not considered any investigation necessary until they were approached by the Civil Aeronautics Board for co-operation. It was unbelievable that a modern jetliner could be sucked upward at great speed without explanation. In the interest of aviation safety the two government bodies joined together to determine what had happened.

Postponements were lengthy and irritating because few scientists could be found who could explain such peculiar atmospheric antics, but four months after the incident, the investigation got under way. Captain Hunt's description of the event was borne out by the flight recorder. This eliminated any doubts that skeptics may have had. The Safety Board finally determined that the United flight had been caught in a weather phenomenon known as an "ascending wave," so powerful that it lifted more than 60 tons of airplane upward at a rate of 2 miles a minute.

As one scientist explained: "This gravitational wave separates itself from other masses of surrounding air and it sneaks in and out of the atmospheric jungle when the ground weather conditions favor the spawning of tornadoes, as was the situation that afternoon in Michigan. They can be compared to the shock wave created on the surface of the ocean by a distant earthquake. The atmospheric shock wave is caused by varying densities of air in motion and when a wave of one density reaches an area above the ground that is less dense, it rushes upward with an anti-gravitational effect. There is usually a spiraling motion of air throughout the district at the time, not unlike a slow-moving tornado unconfined for a few hundred yards and stretching as much as twenty or thirty miles."

The Safety Board was informed that such mysterious waves are not uncommon but rarely interfere with aircraft because they form and die within five minutes, expelling their tremendous energy in a burst of power not unlike a wave breaking upon a beach. These waves cannot be detected or forecast.

The reasonably low weight, as modern jets go, of some 60 tons and the structural integrity of the Boeing 727 may have saved the airliner from breaking up. A Jumbo caught in the same circumstances with a weight of more than 300 tons would have buckled like a frail kite and the cause might never have been discovered.

The ever-present possibility of unpredicted turbulence that does not show on weather radars in the planes or on the ground is the reason why flight attendants would like to have all passengers buckled up during all flights from the moment they board at the airport until they reach their destination and the engines of the aircraft are shut down.

But the law does not support this desire for safety. Seat belts are required to be fastened only during takeoffs and landings, and turbulence has nothing to do with it. The belts are needed at these times in case of a goofed-up landing or an aborted takeoff, which may require sudden emergency braking. Captains usually request that, "for your own safety," the belts be lightly fastened during the entire flight period, and many passengers agree. Yet, people must use the washrooms. Most passengers become nervous during turbulence and are steady customers at the toilets. This is where the danger lies and nothing can be done about it.

The only answer to the turbulence problems is avoidance, using a combination of eyesight, radar, and weather knowledge —a combination found to be lacking in most weather-caused accidents.

13

The One Hundred to One Chance

There are three ways to avoid bad weather: remain on the ground until the bad weather improves, circumnavigate the storm, or fly over it. None of these solutions seems to appeal to pilots or airlines. First a pilot would probably be called "chicken" if he refused to take off and he would have to explain his action to the airline. The second strategy, a circumnavigation, would require permission from Air Traffic Control, and this change in flight plans would create a delay in arrival and the airline would request an explanation. Thirdly, it's not always possible to fly over a storm. The service ceiling of modern jets is 43,000 feet and severe storms have been seen on many occasions as high as 60,000 feet. The U. S. Air Force has even reported a thunderstorm over Puerto Rico up to 120,000 feet. A change in height would require ATC permission, but explanations to the airline would not be required because a change in height rarely causes delays.

Pilots, therefore, continue to fly into storms. They are at the mercy of a forecasting system that has been called the "unexact science." Sophisticated weather reporting fed to airliners from stations along their routes and gathered from hundreds of points in North American relays only probabilities. Pilots, because of lack of professional weather knowledge, will take a chance and fly into storms that do not carry a warning of severity, or have formed so swiftly they have not been reported by other pilots or from surface stations.

This is a deadly trap.

On the evening of December 1, 1974, Northwest Orient Airlines Flight 6231 was operating between Kennedy and Buffalo, where it was to pick up the Baltimore Colts football team. It crashed at 7:26 P.M. Eastern Standard Time, just twelve minutes after takeoff, killing its crew.

The 727 airliner had reached a height of 24,800 feet on its climb toward cruising level at 31,000 feet when it stalled and then dived toward the ground at the incredible speed of 17,000 feet a minute. It slammed into the densely wooded area just west of the village of Thiells, New York. The compact wreckage area of 180 feet by 100 feet indicated that the airliner had plunged straight down.

Captain John B. Lagoria was in command of the jet. He was assisted by First Officer Walter A. Zadra and Second Officer James F. Cox. All three were qualified pilots with a total of more than five thousand hours in the Boeing 727.

Before departing Kennedy, the crew was briefed by Northwest Airlines' meteorology department. From 5 to 7:30 P.M., forecasts showed heavy snow showers from Lake Michigan to the Appalachian Mountains, and moderate to heavy rain showers and scattered thunderstorms east of the Appalachians. At six o'clock the prediction for moderate icing in clouds, locally severe in precipitation above the freezing level, was in effect until eight o'clock, during the period that the flight would be climbing.

Northwest's turbulence plot showed thunderstorms up to a height of 28,000 feet in a triangle formed by Pittsburgh, New York City, and Richmond, Virginia. Since Flight 6231 would be flying north of the New York to Pittsburgh line, the thunderstorms would be of little concern. The weather-reporting station nearest to the crash site was located at Newburgh, New York, 17 miles to the north. At seven that night it reported a ceiling of 2,500 feet with an overcast at 5,000 and a visibility of 12 miles. The ground temperature was 2 degrees above freezing.

Since the ill-fated flight had reported no engine malfunction or other flight problems, the Safety Board came to the conclusion that weather may have played a part in the crash.

The Board first sought to find other aircraft that were in the vicinity that night and interrogate the crews in an effort to determine atmospheric problems, if any. It discovered that another Northwest flight had taken off from New York's La Guardia immediately behind 6231. The captain reported that he had encountered icing and light turbulence during the climb. Because of the decks of clouds piled up to extreme heights, the captain flew under instrument conditions from 1,500 feet to 23,000 feet. This would indicate that the ill-fated flight was in clear air at the time of the stall.

The flight recorder of the crashed 727 disclosed that the flight climbed to 13,500 feet and remained at that altitude for about fifty seconds, during which time the airspeed increased from 264 knots to 304 knots because it was in the level flight as ordered by Air Traffic Control. The aircraft then began to climb 2,500 feet a minute while maintaining an airspeed of about 305 knots. As the altitude increased above 16,000 feet, the "recorded" airspeed began to increase and at the time the first officer commented, "Do you realize we're going 340 knots and I'm climbing at 5,000 feet a minute?" The airliner was behaving more like a bullet than a plane.

The crew discussed the implications of the high airspeed and the high rate of climb. The second officer said, "That's because we're light," after which the captain commented, "It gets up real fast," and "I wish I had my shoulder harness on, it's going to give up pretty soon."

The rate of climb displayed on the altimeter increased to 6,500 feet a minute. As the airliner reached 23,000 feet, the overspeed warning horn sounded. This meant the 727 was exceeding its design speed limit.

"Would you believe that?" commented the captain.

"I believe it; I just can't do anything about it."

"No, just pull her back, let her climb."

This last statement was followed by the sound of a second overspeed warning horn. Ten seconds later the stall warning stick shaker began to wiggle the yoke and the flight was leveled out at 24,800 feet.

The stall warning began again and the first officer commented, "There's that Mach buffet, guess we'll have to pull it up." The captain commanded, "Pull it up." (A slight buffet occurs when an aircraft exceeds its critical Mach number. The buffet is caused by the formation of a shock wave on the wing surfaces and a separation of air flow aft of the shock wave. This change from the smooth air flow to a turbulent flow causes a high-frequency vibration in the control surfaces which is described as "buffet" or "buzz." The aircraft must be slowed down.)

A few seconds after the command to "pull up" the aircraft began to fall and was turning rapidly to the right, indicative of a spin. As the aircraft continued to descend, the downward speed increased dramatically and "mayday" was transmitted. Thirty-three seconds later the crew reported, "We're descending through twelve, we're in a stall." The aircraft's dive increased in speed and the altitude decreased to 1,090 feet—the elevation of the terrain at the accident site. The aircraft had descended from 24,800 feet in eighty-three seconds.

What had happened to a superb aircraft with a good record of dependability? A number of things could have caused the stall—severe turbulence, engine failure, in-flight reversal of engines, the remote possibility of bird ingestion, or the malfunction of flying surfaces. Medical and pathological reports showed that the three crew members died from the impact of the crash; there were no signs of incapacitation from carbon monoxide, hydrogen cyanide, alcohol, or drugs. There was no fire, either during the flight or after the earth-shaking impact.

The Safety Board knew that it would have to reconstruct the flight from the moment of takeoff until the crash. And it would have to move rapidly. With so many 727s in world operations, the tidal wave of concern would not abate until the cause was discovered. Reconstruction of the flight from bits and pieces of wreckage, from salvaged instruments frozen by impact at their last settings, and from the flight and voice recorders would be thorough and painstakingly slow.

As the demolished aircraft was being sifted for clues, the Safety Board was again fortunate to learn of an icing experience by an Eastern Airlines pilot which sounded like a textbook case of what might have happened to the ill-fated Northwest flight.

Captain James A. Hellum was flying a DC-9 back on February 26, 1969, during a milk run along the Atlantic seaboard from Melbourne, Florida, to Montreal, Quebec, when his aircraft entered cloud during one of the climbs and ice began forming on the windshield wipers. He immediately switched on the anti-ice circuitry. His instruments showed that the DC-9 was climbing at about four degrees nose up with maximum and continuous flow of power from the two tail-mounted engines.

Other than the appearance of ice on the windshield wiper, everything seemed to be in order. If ice was accumulating on the leading edges of the wings, the crew would not have been able to see it since the wings are not visible from the flight deck. Suddenly and without any prior warning the overspeed warning horn sounded and this was followed soon afterward by the raucous bellow of the klaxon horn, indicating a stall.

Captain Hellum is known as a "cool cucumber" in the trade. He reviewed his instruments and asked for a corresponding surveillance from his co-pilot. For a few seconds he was unable to determine by the instruments whether he was going up or down. This baffling situation required some swift evaluation and action. He first cut off the circuit breakers that controlled the unnerving horns so that he could think more clearly. Then he concentrated again on the glowing instruments. One of the scores of dials revealed that no current was flowing to the heating elements of the Pitot.

The Pitot is a device familiar to all aviators. It is a long thin tube that juts from the leading edges of the wings to measure velocity and transmits its measurements to the airspeed indicator on the instrument panel of the DC-9 and other multi-engine planes and to a simple dial on small aircraft. Fledgling pilots are repeatedly warned during their training days that the Pitot must be constantly inspected and cleaned. If it becomes clogged, erroneous airspeed readings could result, and this could be disastrous. A fully clogged instrument means that no airspeed will be indicated; partial clogging shows on the instrument panel that airspeed is falling, when in fact the aircraft is maintaining proper airspeed.

In jet airliners this instrument serves the same function as those on small planes but is more sophisticated and contains heating elements to ensure that ice particles do not clog the tiny hole into which air is rammed by the forward motion of the plane.

Captain Hellum saw that the heat was not reaching the Pitot and he turned up the rheostat and in a few seconds the instruments relating to airspeed returned to normal.

Other pilots reported they had icing problems and misreadings of the airspeed indicator. Captain Donald Nelson, chief pilot for Northwest at Minneapolis, recalled he had flown a Boeing 707 off the airport during a snowstorm one night and while passing through an altitude of 400 feet, immediately after takeoff, he was startled to see the airspeed indicator falling, showing a decrease in his climbing speed. However, a few seconds later the altimeter was showing an altitude of 600 feet and he knew then that the airspeed was in error.

When asked why he did not turn on his Pitot heat and melt any ice or snow accumulation, Captain Nelson replied that the Boeing 707 was not equipped with Pitot heaters because Boeing engineers had placed the Pitots in "protected areas" where ice and snow were not supposed to interfere with their operation.

As the inquiry continued, Northwest Airlines told the Safety Board that all pre-flight checking procedures call for the mandatory switch of the Pitot heat to "On" as soon as the engines are started and a recheck of the system is necessary before taxiing to the active runway for the takeoff.

The Board discovered in the tangle of wreckage that was once the instrument and engineering panel that "contrary to standard operational procedures, the flight crew had not activated the Pitot heaters. Evidence in this case indicates the heaters were capable of operation," the Board stated.

Checking with procedures of other airlines, the Board found

that some carriers insist that Pitots be turned on during all flights, bad weather or not. Carriers who did not insist on this procedure quickly changed their operation manuals to include mandatory "On" for the heaters during every future flight.

What bothered the investigating team of the Safety Board was the plain fact that an inexpensive heater that was not activated should cause a fatal problem in a modern 727 jet, the most popular aircraft in the world.

A survey of operators showed a casual concern over icing conditions, because jets fly so rapidly through atmospheric icing conditions that accumulations are insufficient to cause problems in the flight and control surfaces. Experiments had shown that during a climb through an average 6,500-foot layer of cloud, only an inch or so of ice would be deposited on the leading edges of Boeing 707s and 720s, on which the tests were made. The 727 climbs even more rapidly than its sister jets.

"Since icing is encountered only about once in a hundred flights," the Boeing report said, "some 7,500 pounds of fuel are expended to carry a system that might be used once. On this one flight which encounters icing, the chances are ten to one against ice building up to a thickness that would develop as much drag as the fuel penalty for the added weight of the de-icing system on that flight. Thus on a thousand flights averaging 2,000 miles each, 75,000 pounds of fuel are expended to carry an unnecessary system."

But that icing encounter, though only once in a hundred flights, bothered the Safety Board, and it recommended to the FAA that a system be installed on all transport aircraft that would indicate by a warning light when the Pitot system was not operating, and to amend the Federal Air Regulations to require the Pitot heating system to be activated anytime that electrical power is applied to the aircraft.

But the FAA did not agree.

Acting Administrator James E. Dow replied: "We do not concur in this recommendation. Some current aircraft have cycling types of Pitot heaters. These cycle on and off as controlled by thermostats and timers. Warning lights would flash off and on. We consider this as distracting and possibly detrimental to safety."

As for the safety recommendation that heaters be on during every flight, the FAA made the following comment: "We do not consider the recommendation practical for general adoption. Some cyclic installations will not tolerate continuous heat. Continuous heat would make it unsafe in many circumstances."

The Safety Board determined that the probable cause of the loss of control of the 727 was due to the crew's failure to analyze the problem and correct the aircraft's high angle of attack (climb), low speed stall, and descending spiral.

The stall was precipitated by the "crew's improper reaction to the erroneous airspeed, which had resulted from the blockage of the Pitot heads by atmospheric icing." There was no recommendation by the Safety Board to the FAA on this occasion to install ice-warning instruments on jets. In the old days, piston-engine aircraft moved ponderously into icing conditions and blocks of ice built up on the wings and on the tail surfaces. Heating units and de-icing boots flexed away the accumulation. But in designing jets, engineers agreed that the high-speed characteristics would carry the aircraft through icing in a matter of seconds. There would no longer be a threat. Cumbersome and expensive de-icing equipment therefore would not be required on the new breed of airliners.

But if the high speed of modern planes was expected to carry crew and passengers safely through icing conditions, the precise opposite would occur when the jets flew into hail, which is often associated with thunderstorms.

Hail is perhaps the most important reason why jets should avoid thunderstorms by a wide margin. "If you can see the thunderhead, stay clear," is a storm warning for all fledgling pilots. A refresher course on the subject may be necessary for pilots and air traffic controllers if safety is to be improved.

Thunderstorms contain massive updrafts of hot, humid air that ascend to great heights at speeds up to 5,000 feet a minute. As this upward draft enters the cold region between 20,000 and 40,000 feet, the moisture in the cell condenses first into rain and then into ice crystals.

The upward and downward motion of air forms a cell of tremendous energy, upward on the inside and downward on the outside, often compacted to within a space of several hundred yards (a small one) or as wide as several miles. Some of the ascending air rockets to the top of the cell structure and is caught by the high-altitude winds and forms the familiar anvil appearance. From the protuberance of the anvil hail forms and descends with great rapidity.

After passing through or bypassing a cell, an airliner can run directly into the pathway of the descending hail. If the radar shows a hooked finger sticking out from the cell's perimeter, a tornado or a hail cloud is present. But hail itself is not visible on the radar—it shows only as precipitation.

The pilot uses his radar to fly between the echoes of precipitation. Echoes are the returning messages when radar signals are repulsed by solids and bounce back. Raindrops with their nuclei of dust form a solid reflection to the scanning radar beams and return the signal to the screen. Therefore, the pilot "sees the precipitation" and attempts to work his aircraft between the densest of the echoes. But often behind the wall of the heaviest precipitation lurk the most dangerous cells, the killer tornadoes, the lethal turbulence, and the hail.

The lessons on hail go back far enough. In May 1959 the industry was warned by the magazine *Flight Comment*, a publication of the Royal Canadian Air Force containing a feature article entitled "Safety Is Your Business."

"The damage that hail will do to an aircraft depends upon two factors: the size of the stones and the speed of the aircraft," reported the RCAF, and embellished the statement with photos of a smashed windshield on a jet transport, dents on the jet air intakes which could interfere with air flow to the engines, and a damaged compressor within the engine complex.

Listing experiments made by the United States Civil Aeronautics Authority, the RCAF reported that experiments made with three-quarter-inch hailstones fired at 225 knots against a piston-engine aircraft made no measurable indentation. One-

and-one-quarter-inch stones fired at the same speed made indentations of $\frac{4}{100}$ of an inch.

"With jet aircraft, however, with their high airspeed, even half-inch stones can be damaging and big stones very dangerous," it was reported. "The nose section, the leading edges of the wings and tail, cowlings, radar domes and jet engines may be affected—not only the cowlings but also the compressor where damage may result from hail ingestion."

The RCAF was warning the industry of the damage that could be created by hailstones of one half to one and one quarter inches in diameter. The caution may have gone unnoticed. But there was soon to be an alarming aftermath to the RCAF admonition.

14

Hail Was as Big as Baseballs

On the stormy afternoon of Monday, April 4, 1977, the hail-stones that were falling over the northwest section of Georgia were as large as baseballs when they struck the ground. They would be considerably larger higher up in the sky along the jet pathways leading to Atlanta's busy airport.

Captain William McKenzie and First Officer Lyman Keele had encountered a "mile or two" of hail while flying through storm conditions between Atlanta and Huntsville, Alabama, about 2:30 P.M. that day and were queried by the Huntsville controller about the weather along their route.

"Is it raining in Atlanta?" asked the controller.

"No, sir, not yet," the crew reported from Southern Airways' Flight 245.

Then the tower controller said: "They've had some tornadoes reported about halfway between here and there."

Pilots McKenzie and Keele did not reply to this comment. They landed at Huntsville and then continued on to Muscle Shoals, Alabama. For the return trip to Atlanta, the flight became number 242 and departed Muscle Shoals for Huntsville.

Prior to the return flight from Muscle Shoals, Captain McKenzie and First Officer Keele were briefed by Southern Airways' flight personnel on the general weather of the area which disclosed a warm front running from Indiana to North

Carolina and behind it a rampaging squall line that involved parts of Georgia, Tennessee, and Mississippi. The teletype machines were churning out warnings of thunderstorm weather along Flight 242's route with thunder and lightning already in progress over Huntsville. However, the flight arrived at Huntsville uneventfully and there is no evidence that the crew was given a weather briefing at this point.

Yet at 1:17 P.M. a tornado watch had been issued by the National Severe Storms Forecast Center at Kansas City, Missouri, for a portion of east Tennessee, northeast Alabama, and northern Georgia, warning there was a possibility of tornadoes and severe thunderstorms with large hail and damaging winds.

From two o'clock until 6 P.M. the watch area included a 140-mile stretch from 50 miles southwest of Chattanooga, Tennessee, to 30 miles northeast of Hickory, North Carolina, across Southern's flight path.

There could be no doubt about the significance of the warning and the sinister events already taking place in the area. At one o'clock, Union Grove, Alabama, reported a tornado. This and all other reports to follow were teletyped on the military teletypewriter network to all weather stations and airports in the vicinity.

At 1:15 P.M., a tornado was reported at 37 miles north of Gadsden, Alabama. Fifty minutes later, another funnel was observed at Ragland, Alabama, and twenty minutes later yet another twister at Falkville, just 20 miles south of Huntsville. At 2:55 P.M., hail, one and three quarter inches in diameter, was found at Warrior, Alabama, 15 miles northwest of Birmingham. Within minutes, tornadoes were reported at Birmingham and Gadsden. At 4:45 P.M., a black twister was seen in Murray County, Georgia, approximately 30 miles southeast of Chattanooga. This latter observation would place the tornadoes along Southern's flight path from Huntsville to Atlanta.

Tornadoes, however, are not considered dangerous to jets because they fly above the low storm squalls that spawn them. Landing and taking off in such weather conditions are considered dangerous, although flights were arriving at and departing Atlanta that afternoon despite the warnings and the approaching black clouds.

As the Southern flight approached Huntsville for the brief stop to take on the Atlanta-bound passengers, controller Raymond Harber seated at the later screen of his Approach Control position had his range set at 40 miles and reported to Captain McKenzie the area of bad weather. On landing, McKenzie would see the warning bulletins pouring off the teletypes from New Orleans to Washington and from Miami to Atlanta.

Valid at that time was a flight precaution warning of thunderstorms to above 40,000 feet with a line running through Georgia containing numerous thunderstorms, a few of them severe, and possible tornadoes. From Miami came a National Weather Service warning of flight precautions specifically for Atlanta, where severe thunderstorms were developing and containing hail and strong wind gusts.

This ferocity in the sky had by now killed twenty-one persons as village after village was reduced to rubble. Northwestern Georgia and northeastern Alabama were no places to be on that wild and stormy afternoon. Between Muscle Shoals and Huntsville, a United Airlines flight about this time decided that the weather was not fit for flying and turned around to return to another base. However, none of this deterred Captain McKenzie from taking his DC-9 off Huntsville Runway 18-Right at 3:52 P.M. Aboard were sixty persons.

Two minutes later, Huntsville's Departure Control advised Southern 242 to make left turns to avoid a restricted storm area and to climb and maintain 17,000 feet altitude and hold direct course to a radio point known as Rome just west of the William B. Hartsfield Atlanta International Airport.

At this time the departure controller said: "Southern two forty-two, I'm painting a line of weather which appears to be moderate to possibly heavy precipitation starting about five miles ahead and it's approximately fifteen miles in width."

The flight replied that it was in rain, and what was pointed out to them didn't look much heavier than the weather they were in at the present time.

Having a longer range and a more powerful radar set than that in the DC-9, the departure controller differed with Southern, reporting that the storm ahead of it was a "bit heavier than you're in now." At this time the Huntsville controller handed the flight over to Memphis Center, but not before informing the flight that the path ahead would not get any worse than the moderate rain and turbulence being reported. Southern was at 9,000 feet and still climbing.

Precisely eight seconds after switching frequency from Huntsville to Memphis, the following statement was made to all aircraft under Memphis control: ATTENTION ALL AIRCRAFT. SIGMET. (Significant weather to the safety of all aircraft.) HAZARDOUS WEATHER VICINITY TENNESSEE SOUTHEASTERN LOUISIANA MISSISSIPPI NORTHERN AND WESTERN ALABAMA AND ADJACENT COASTAL WATERS MONITOR THE VOR BROADCAST WITHIN ONE HUNDRED AND FIFTY MILE RADIUS OF THIS SIGMET AREA.

Flight SO242 was told to contact the Atlanta Air Traffic Control Center. The time was now two minutes and fifty-three seconds after four o'clock. One minute later the flight reported it had reached its assigned altitude of 17,000 feet and two minutes eleven seconds later radioed that it was "slowing up a bit."

At this point, computer information on the flight showed that its ground speed was reduced from 412 knots to 354 knots and the flight was ordered to start down and decrease its height to 14,000 feet. The clock at 4:07 P.M. showed Southern at 17,500 feet—but *rising*. Fourteen seconds later Southern was at 18,300 feet. Ten seconds later it had dropped to 17,000 feet and the groundspeed was 374 knots.

This violent change in altitude would indicate that Southern had flown into a thunderstorm cell where the ascending winds were so powerful that the airliner could be moved 800 feet upward in fourteen seconds.

During an agonizing period of silence, Atlanta Center received a report from a TWA jet that severe turbulence and heavy precipitation were being troublesome, but the controller handling the flights offered a balmy reassurance that 15 miles ahead the weather was "a little better."

"Okay, good to have hope anyway," reported the TWA flight.

The ATC commented: "Well, looks like you might, uh, went [sic] through a little one over there and, uh, looks like you oughta be out of it now, though."

"Ah, we're painting a little one but, ah, you know you wouldn't let us go any further, so we're sorta in a box." (A thunderstorm cell is referred to as a painting. The captain was saying that he had been denied a chance to avoid the cell by changing his course.)

Center: "Well, I have another airplane out over there [Southern] to your left-hand side too—the reason why you can't get on the other way."

TWA: "I know, but it is just too narrow through here."

Center: "Yeah—he'd be a lot harder than a cloud, though."

The reply referring to the "cloud, though" indicated that ATC was routing the TWA between cells, but it obviously was not successful since the flight passed through a "little one." That reply shows a clear insensitivity to the situation.

The Center next gave the Atlanta airport altimeter reading, a routine procedure for inbound flights. Southern was told to cross a beacon 40 miles northwest of Atlanta at a precise speed of 250 knots. A minute and a half later the flight reported that the airspeed had been reduced but asked Center to "stand by."

"We just got our windshield busted," the flight reported twenty-seven seconds later. "We'll, and uh, try and get it back up to fifteen . . . we're at fourteen."

This conversation made it obvious that McKenzie had descended according to instructions but may have run into hail which broke his one-and-a-half-inch-thick windshield. He wanted to climb up now to get away from what he thought was a dangerous level. If there was another reason for his request, it may never be known. (Discussing the request, air traffic controllers far away from the Atlanta region believed that the Southern pilot was not trying to escape the hail but was attempting to get above severe turbulence after the hail attack. He may have still been in a cell.)

The windshield could have broken as a result of a sudden change in pressure between the airliner and the outside atmosphere, a pressure ratio so severe that it could only be compared with the extreme low pressure in a dangerous thunderstorm cell or a tornado. Because of the height, the tornado idea was dismissed, leaving a single cell as the possible culprit.

From the tower tape recorder, the conversations between Air Route Traffic Control Center (ARTCC) and Southern Atlanta Approach Control (TAR-2), and Atlanta Tower (ATL) sounded like this:

ARTCC: Southern two forty-two, you say you're at fourteen now.

Southern: Er, couldn't help it.

ARTCC: Roger, that's okay, uh, are you squawking five six two three? [The controller is reporting that the transponder is not being received on its assigned frequency. This is sometimes an indication of an electrical problem or that precipitation is so intense that no signals are getting through.]

Southern: Our left engine just cut out.

ARTCC: Southern two forty-two, roger. Uh, I've lost your transponder, squawk five six two three.

Southern: Five six two three, we've squawking.

ARTCC: You say you've lost an engine and, uh, busted the windshield?

Southern: Yes, sir.

ARTCC: Southern two four two, you can descend and maintain one three thousand [13,000 feet] now; that'll get you down a little lower.

Southern: That's the other engine going too. [There are only two engines on a DC-9 and the captain is reporting that all the power has been lost. The airliner must now glide toward the ground at a speed that will prevent a stall and a spin.]

The air route controller phoned Atlanta Tower and Atlanta Approach Control, informing them that Southern had lost the two engines. An incredulous controller at Approach called back: "He has no engines? Put him on me and we'll land him at Dobbins."

Dobbins Air Force Base was located approximately 10 miles to the left of Southern's flight path to the Atlanta runway.

ARTCC: Say it again.

Southern: Stand by, we've lost both engines—give us a vector to a clear area, Atlanta.

ARTCC: Roger. Continue your present southeastbound heading—there's a TWA off to your left about fourteen miles at fourteen thousand and says he's in the clear.

Southern: Okay. [The time was precisely 1610.18, ten minutes and eighteen seconds after four o'clock.]

ARTCC: Southern two forty-two, contact Approach Control on one two six point niner, they'll try to—uh—land you at Dobbins. [It seems unreasonable to ask the flight to change its radio frequency at a time when the pilots would be trying desperately to restart the engines and maintain as shallow a glide angle as possible to gain distance without diving into the ground. The pilots could not have known that both engines had been so badly damaged within the turbine section that they could never be restarted. A similar switching of frequency during an emergency occurred at Toronto International Airport on July 5, 1970, when immediately after an Air Canada DC-8 struck the runway on landing and wrenched an engine loose, the tower controller, seeing the aircraft attempting a takeoff for a "go-around," instructed the flight to switch to Departure Control. No sooner was this done than the tower noticed fire streaming from beneath the wings and was unable to reach the flight. The plane exploded 5 miles farther out and 109 persons died. Had the tower controller kept the flight under his control without switching it to another controller, the crew could have been alerted to the fire and would have had more than two minutes to pancake the giant airliner into the fields directly ahead. It flew for another 42,000 feet before blowing up.]

The Air Route Traffic Control Center is located at Hampton, Georgia, about 20 miles south of Atlanta airport. The Approach Control Center is located below the tower on the airport property. There are a number of controllers on duty here guiding planes into Atlanta from various points of the compass, and by pushing a particular button, they can talk to any of the other controllers on duty, to the center at Hampton, or to the staff in the glass-enclosed tower above them. As an example of how they work the system, the approach controller working Southern 242 and desiring to have the nearby TWA flight assist the stricken airliner would have to call the controller working the TWA flight and that controller would have to call Air

Route Traffic Control to get a change of height to bring the TWA lower down to observe and assist the Southern. At a critical period, which now faced all these controllers involved, the conversations back and forth snipped away precious seconds.

In this instance Air Route Traffic Control should have declared an emergency, and cleared all approaching aircraft. Then all the controllers could have used an open line to get the Southern either to the closest airport or to put him on the nearest of the expressways which trace a broad and unencumbered network northwest of Atlanta. But according to the rules, only the captain of the airliner can declare an emergency, no matter how obvious the seriousness of the problem is to the controllers. If the transponder is squawking an emergency and cannot be seen by the controllers and the captain is too busy trying to save the plane to declare the emergency, the seriousness of the situation increases.

As a result of this confusion, the chance to get Southern into Cartersville Airport, which was the nearest to the flight at the time, was missed. Dobbins Air Force Base, a satellite to Atlanta airport, is large enough to handle the biggest planes and has a tower controller on duty at all times. The airport is adjacent to the city of Marietta, Georgia, 15 miles from Atlanta airport. Dobbins was the best airport. But it was not the closest by any means.

Approach Control called Dobbins Tower, whose identification is MGE:

ATL: I got a Southern DC-9, he is eight miles, make that twelve miles, to the northwest of you at the present time, he's got both engines out and we're going to be landing your runway, if that's okay.

MGE: Okay. Could I have his call sign?

ATL: Yes, sir, it's Southern two forty-two.

MGE: He's uh, DC.

ATL: I'll call you back some more information on this.

MGE: All right.

ATL to ARTCC: He's got a vector to Dobbins . . . I'm not talking to him . . . I've got radar with him but I've lost his beacon. [No coded transponder. Both Air Route

Traffic Control and Approach Control start calling the
Southern flight. There is no response. ATL receives a call
from another controller monitoring the northwest section
and identified as ZTL.]

ZTL: Yeah, I have too.

TWA pilots try to reach Southern: Two forty-two, do you read
TWA?

There is no response.

ATL: Southern—it looks like he's spinning out there. [In controller jargon, the Southern flight has made a 360-degree
turn.]

ZTL: If that primary is him—you still not talking to him?
[Primary is radar image.]

ATL: We are not talking to him.

ZTL: Okay, we can't reach him either.

ATL: Will you hit him on guard and see if he's listening? [On
guard is the emergency frequency of 121.5.]

At thirteen minutes and nine seconds after the hour, Southern calls in to Atlanta Approach Control and the signal is immediately answered by a controller identified as TAR-2.

TAR-2: Atlanta Approach . . . go ahead.

Southern: Uh, we've lost both engines—how about giving us a
vector to the nearest place—we're at seven thousand feet.

TAR-2: Southern two forty-two, roger, turn right, heading of
one zero zero vectors to Dobbins for straight-in approach
runway one one, altimeter two niner five two—your position is fifteen, correction, twenty miles west of Dobbins at
this time.

Southern: 'Kay, uh, one forty heading and twenty miles.

TAR-2: Uh, make a heading of one two zero, Southern two
forty-two, right turn to one two zero.

Southern: Okay, right turn to one two zero and, uh, you got
us on our squawk, haven't you—on emergency? [The co-
pilot Lyman Keele is handling the radio and the captain is
flying the aircraft.]

TAR-2: I'm not receiving it but radar contact your position is
twenty miles west of Dobbins.

Southern: 'Kay.

TAR-2: Delta seven fifty-nine, contact Approach Control one
two seven point two five now.

TAR-2: Eastern six eighty-three, contact Approach Control one two seven point two five.

Eastern: Six eighty-three.

TAR-2: Eastern one forty-three [another Eastern on approach], reduce speed to one seven zero knots.

TAR-2: Eastern six eleven [another Eastern flight], reduce speed to two one zero knots.

TAR-2: TWA five eighty-four, descend and maintain one one thousand, you can expect an ILS runway two six, altimeter is two nine five two, localizer frequency one zero eight point seven. [Approach is guiding the TWA to the radio localizer where the turn will be made into the active runway.]

TWA: Five eight four out of fourteen for eleven, roger.

Southern: (Unintelligible) . . . I . . . I can't tell . . . tell you, uh, the implication of this, uh, we, uh, only got two engines and how far is Dobbins now? [It would appear that Southern doesn't think that Approach Control realizes the seriousness of the situation—a plane with only two engines and neither working.]

TAR-2: Southern, uh, two forty-two, uh, nineteen miles.

Southern: We're out of, uh, fifty-eight hundred two hundred knots. [Southern is dropping rapidly, approximately about 23.3 feet per second or 1,400 feet a minute.]

TAR-2: Southern two forty-two, do you have one engine running now?

Southern: Negative—no engines.

TAR-2: Ah, roger.

TAR-2: (Two seconds later) Eastern one forty-three, fly heading of one nine zero.

TAR-2: (Twenty seconds later) Eastern six eleven, reduce speed to one seven zero knots.

Eastern 611: Slowing.

Southern: What's your Dobbins weather?

TAR-2: Stand by.

TAR-2: (Seven seconds later) TWA five eight four, reduce speed to one seven zero knots.

TWA 584: Seventy-five eighty-four.

TAR-2: (Twenty-eight seconds after Southern's weather query) Southern uh, two forty-two, the Dobbins weather is two thousand scattered estimated ceiling three thousand broken, seven thousand overcast, visibility seven miles. [Southern cannot see the airport and is obviously flying in broken storm cloud conditions.]

Southern: Okay, we're down to forty-six now.

TAR-2: Ah, roger, and you're approximately, uh, seventeen miles west of Dobbins at this time.

Southern: Don't know whether we can make that or not.

TAR-2: Ah, roger.

TAR-2: Eastern one forty-three contact Approach Control one two seven point two five.

TAR-2: Eastern six eleven, reduce speed to one seven zero knots.

Eastern 611: We're doing six eleven. What is he—a Martin or a con, uh, nine?

TAR-2: DC nine.

Southern: (Sixteen minutes, twenty-five seconds after the hour) Is any airport between our position and Dobbins, uh?

TAR-2: Southern two forty-two, uh, no, sir, closest airport is Dobbins. [*Wrong.*]

Southern: I doubt if we're going to make it, but we're trying everything to get something started. [Still trying to start the engine that cannot be started—ever.]

TAR-2: Ah, roger, well, there is Cartersville, you're approximately ten miles south of Cartersville, fifteen miles west of Dobbins.

Southern: Give us a vector to Cartersville.

TAR-2: All right, turn left heading of three six zero, be directly, uh, direct vector to Cartersville.

Southern: Three six zero, roger—what's the runway heading?

TAR-2: Stand by.

Southern: How long is it?

TAR-2: Stand by.

TAR-2: Eastern one forty-three, contact Approach Control one two seven point two five.

TAR-2: TWA five eighty-four, turn left leading one one zero.

TWA 584: Ah, hundred and ten degrees, five eighty-four.

TAR-2: Eastern six eleven, uh, reduce speed to one seven zero knots and contact Approach Control one two seven point two five now.

TAR-2: Southern, uh, two forty-two, the, uh, runway

configuration at Cartersville is, uh, three six zero and one eighty north and south, and, uh, the elevation is seven hundred and fifty-six feet and, uh, I'm trying to get the length now—three thousand two hundred feet long.

Southern: (Eighteen minutes and three seconds after the hour) We're putting it down on a highway—we're down to nothing.

TAR-2: Putting it down on the highway. Roger. (Eight seconds later) Southern two forty-two, Atlanta surface weather one nine zero at two five.

This was the last known communication with the flight. The precise time according to the flight recorder readout was eighteen minutes and fourteen seconds after four o'clock. The flight had another nineteen seconds of life.

Ahead of it, gleaming like a ribbon of hope between the pine forests that sprang from Georgia's rust-red sand, appeared a main highway to the eager eyes of the flight crew. There was no other choice but to attempt to set the DC-9 on that highway. It descended from 500 feet to 300 feet quickly and a number of motorists on Georgia Highway 92, at the outskirts of the village of New Hope, swung their cars off the highway to miss being struck by the aircraft. The wheels were in the down position and the flaps on the wings had been extended as in a normal landing pattern for an airport.

One driver sped up to get ahead of the plane in the rearview mirror. The aircraft passed over him, however, but at that moment the wings began clipping trees. Captain McKenzie was apparently trying to make a clearing about a quarter of a mile ahead of him. But time had run out. The village of New Hope was coming under the wings as the DC-9 shuddered from its first impact with the trees. A grocery store disappeared in a flaming explosion of gasoline from its service station tanks. A car parked outside the store, in which a mother and her two youngsters were seated, dissolved like jelly in a blast of searing heat.

Persons inside their cottages thought that a tornado had struck the village. They had been hearing about tornadoes all that day. (At Kansas City the Severe Storms Center was pre-

*Pilots of this Southern Airways
DC-9 crash-landed into the
village of New Hope, Georgia,
during a severe thunderstorm.*
(Associated Press)

*With both engines knocked out
by the fury of the elements,
the stricken DC-9 claimed the
lives of sixty-two in the plane and
eight on the ground.*
(Associated Press)

A KLM Flying Dutchman (above) and a Pan Am Clipper (below)—both Boeing 747s—collided on the fog-shrouded runway of Tenerife, in the Canary Islands, killing 579 persons.

The fire-ravaged shell is all that remains of the KLM 747, the world's largest airliner. (Associated Press)

The stark monument to the world's worst aircraft disaster is the undercarriage of the Pan Am Clipper at Tenerife. (Associated Press)

Into the Yugoslav cornfields near Zagreb the passengers and crews of two airliners fell like birds after the worst mid-air collision in a half century of flight. An air traffic controller was found guilty of criminal negligence and was sentenced to seven years in jail. (Associated Press)

Air traffic controllers around the world rely on this typical radar screen to shepherd aircraft along the highways of the sky.

paring to issue a tornado warning for that very area, to be expected in two hours' time.) Mrs. Marie Clayton, working in her front yard with her two daughters, was watching the storm which was appearing to build up.

"I heard a big roaring sound," she said. "I screamed for everyone to run and I looked down the highway and here was coming a jet plane. It hit Mr. Newman's store and killed his daughter and his two grandchildren. It was breaking apart down the road. It was throwing pieces up in the air and they were exploding.

"I ran into my house with my kids and tried to use the phone but it wouldn't work. I ran out and started helping people who were hurt and saw forty or fifty people lying on the ground and not moving. I ran and got some sheets to put over them."

Captain McKenzie and his co-pilot were dead. So were sixty others on the plane and eight on the ground. Twenty-five survived when they were hurled out of the disintegrating aircraft.

Frederick Clemens, eighteen, of Wilmington, Delaware, was one of the passengers who survived. He was burned on 20 per cent of his body. "We were flying through a hailstorm and I guess the hailstones clogged up the engine or something," he related. "After that we had three or four minutes with both the jet engines blown, and we coasted down to a forced landing, and all I remember was when we started hitting it was getting rougher."

John Clayton, chief of the New Hope Volunteer Fire Department, said he was in his back yard when he thought he heard a tornado coming and turned to look. He saw the plane.

"It dipped first, and came down before it got to New Hope," he recalled. "Then it got airborne again and then it touched down and one of the first things it clipped were the telephone poles and the electrical power lines of the Fire Department. Then the grocery store and vehicles, and then it started clipping the trees. The fuselage at that point in front of Mrs. Irene Craton's and Ruth Bell's house turned a somersault and landed in the yard of Mr. Meory Burkhalter, directly across from my home.

"We actually saw the fuselage slipping, the wings disintegrating, and bodies—bodies going through the air, debris, all kinds of articles being flung from the airliner. I saw twenty-five lifeless bodies then," he said.

Rudy Kaupstin, chief investigator for the Safety Board assigned to the crash, said when he arrived at the death site: "The biggest question right now is how Southern was allowed to get into a weather system that had given good evidence of severe weather."

But then, bad weather is the cause of 15 per cent of all air accidents and 38 per cent of all fatal accidents.

On September 16, some five months after the crash, the National Transportation Safety Board issued the following recommendations to the FAA:

(1) Require that each Air Traffic Control facility depict on the map portion of its radar displays those airports immediately outside of that facility's jurisdiction.

(2) Expedite the development and implementation of an aviation weather subsystem for both en route and terminal area environments which is capable of providing a real-time display of either precipitation or turbulence, or both, and which includes a multiple intensity classification scheme, and transmit this information to pilots either via the controllers as a safety advisory, or on electronic data link-up.

(3) Establish a standard scale of thunderstorm intensity based on national weather services on a six-level scale, and promote its widespread use as a common language to describe thunderstorms and precipitation intensity. Additionally, indoctrinate pilots and Air Traffic Control personnel in the use of this system.

(4) Transmit Sigmets more frequently on Navaids so that pilots can secure more timely information about hazardous weather.

(5) Code to geographical applicability Severe Thunderstorm Watch bulletins and Severe Tornado Watch bulletins from Severe Storms Warning centers.

If adopted, these recommendations would provide pilots with up-to-the-minute reports of storm intensity along their prescribed routes either by direct contact from controllers or by weather reports directed for all aircraft using stormy routes. The geographical display on radar of satellite airports in the vicinity of a major airport would permit controllers to know precisely the relationship of an aircraft to its nearest airport and in time of emergency could expedite a landing with all the knowledge of the airport runways and elevation instantly available.

The NTSB might have gone further and recommended the geographical display of major limited-access highways beneath flightpaths in case satellite airports were not close enough for a stricken aircraft.

PART IV

The Human Factor

15

Preoccupation in the Cockpit

A textbook case of what causes preoccupation in the cockpit occurred on December 29, 1972, and should be included in a course study for all airline pilots. On that balmy moonless night, Eastern Airlines Flight 401 was en route to Miami from New York with 176 aboard. As the Lockheed 1011 approached the Miami control area it was ordered to descend to 9,000 feet to a point about 30 miles west of Miami over the Everglades.

Then, under the guidance of the approach controller, the flight was brought down to an elevation of 1,700 feet. The wind was 7 knots on the nose and the temperature was a soft 72 degrees. Captain Robert Loft, a fifty-five-year-old veteran with Eastern, lined his giant aircraft on a heading of 103 degrees bound for Runway 19-Left and switched his radio frequency to the Miami Tower, where the controller had Eastern visibly in sight.

The flight crew then turned to the mandatory check-out of all systems for the landing estimated at nine minutes away.

Second Officer Donald Repo, fifty-one, an engineer who had been with Eastern since 1947, confirmed that ignition on all three engines was continuous and began to call out the check list.

"No smoke," said the engineer, referring to the "No Smoking" signs, and the captain replied crisply, "Coming on."

"Brake system."

"Okay."

"Radar."

"Up and off." (There was a sound of a click. Weather radar is not needed on the landing and turning it off lessens confusion on the panel.)

"Hydraulic panels checked?" the engineer asked.

"Thirty-five . . . thirty-three," responded First Officer Albert Stockstill, thirty-nine, the co-pilot.

"Engine cross-speeds are open," the engineer reported and asked if the landing gear was down.

"No nose gear," responded the co-pilot.

"I gotta raise it back up," replied the captain, thinking it had not fully descended.

The sound of the flap position warning horn began and the flaps were engaged.

"I'm going to try it one more time," said the captain, referring to the nose gear.

"All right," replied the first officer just as the altitude alert horn sounded at about 1,300 feet.

The nose gear indicator did not respond to the repeated attempts by the captain to lower the system. He called the tower and reported that he would have to circle again while he tried to get the gear cleared.

"Eastern four zero one, roger, pull up . . . climb straight ahead to two thousand, go back to Approach Control on one twenty-eight six."

"Twenty-two degrees," said the first officer, making his turn to the northeast over Hialeah. "Gear up?"

"Put power on it first, Bert, thata boy," said the captain. "Leave the gear lever down until we find out what we got."

"All right."

"Do you want me to test the lights or not?" asked the engineer.

"Yeah."

"Bob, it might be the light, jiggle it, it's gotta come out a little bit, and then snap it in, we're up at two thousand. You want me to fly it, Bob?"

"What frequency did he want us on, Bert?" asked the captain before replying to his co-pilot.

"One twenty-eight six."

"I'll talk to 'im."

Meanwhile the engineer, looking into the maze of lights and instruments, asked: "It's right above that . . . ah . . . red one . . . is it not?"

"Yeah. Oh, I can't get it from here," replied the captain.

"I can't make it pull out either," answered the engineer.

"Have we got pressure?"

"Yes, sir, all systems."

Less than six minutes had elapsed since the beginning of the first approach.

"Put it on auto-pilot," ordered the captain.

"Okay," replied co-pilot Stockstill.

"See if you can get that light pulled out."

"All right."

"Now push the switches, just forward."

"Okay."

"You gotta turn it sideways then . . . naw. I don't think it'll fit . . . You gotta turn it one quarter to the left."

Miami Approach called: "Eastern four zero one, turn left to heading three zero zero."

Captain: "Okay."

Ten seconds after this acknowledgment, Captain Loft asked his co-pilot to leave his seat and climb down through the hatch to see if the nosewheel was suspended, but Stockstill was still trying to pull the light bulb from the socket. He asked for a handkerchief or some Kleenex, saying that if he could cushion the bulb with a pair of pliers he could get it out. Then he would replace it. But again both the engineer and the co-pilot found the bulb too stubborn to be removed.

After talking to the Miami Tower and changing his course slightly, Captain Loft finally said: "To hell with it . . . Go down and see if it's lined up with that red line . . . That's all we care . . . go-around because of that, a twenty-cent piece of light equipment we got on this thing."

"Ha ha ha," came the sound of laughter over the system.

"How much fuel we got left on this thing?" asked the captain, noting they had been airborne two hours and eighteen minutes out of New York.

"Fifty-two five . . . It won't come out, no way," replied Stockstill, referring to the slippery bulb.

Finally the engineer slipped below the cockpit floor and was joined by an unnamed employee of Eastern who had been riding the jump seat. They were going to determine if the nose gear had dropped and had locked.

The airliner purred eastward at 174 knots as set by the automatic pilot. The altimeter showed the height to be 1,900 feet. But seconds later the altimeter dropped to 1,855 feet.

Captain Loft was so preoccupied with the nose gear problem that he must have overlooked the falling numerals on the altimeter, believing that the automatic pilot would keep it at the prescribed height. The altitude warning light was not flashing because it doesn't engage under 2,500 feet.

Suddenly the altitude C-chord sounded the alert with its one-second bleeps. But the captain, apparently leaning over to get an answer from below the hatch, whose opening had increased the sound of air flow into the cockpit, did not hear the bleeps.

The 1011 was sinking lower and lower. The crew was not aware of it. Neither were the passengers. There are no reference lights over the Everglades. It was pitch black below.

The co-pilot returned to his position, apparently convinced that the nosewheel was engaged, and yelled, wanting to know what had happened to the altitude.

"What?" gasped the captain. The radio altimeter sounded its alarm. "What's happening here?"

Captain Loft would never know.

Three seconds later he was dead.

The Jumbo slammed into the swamp. Screams of passengers and the shriek of tearing metal filled the silence. The left engine was torn off. The main landing gear was swept into the swamp water and bounced away like a cork. The plane disintegrated over the next 1,600 feet, scattering wreckage and humans some 150 feet to either side. The fuselage broke into four main sections but mercifully for those who would survive, the swamp water prevented the outbreak of a fuel explosion. One small fire erupted and burned fourteen trapped passengers. But it also helped later by serving as a beacon for a search and rescue mission.

A broken instrument panel clock was stopped a few seconds after 11:42 P.M., marking precisely the time of the first crash of a Jumbo jet in passenger service. A total of 101 persons were dead or dying. Miraculously 75 persons lived.

Dead in the crash was First Officer Stockstill. But engineer Repo and the unnamed helper in the nose cavity lived. Two of the ten stewardesses aboard died.

An autopsy upon the captain disclosed a brain tumor which emanated from the right side of the sensorium and displaced and thinned the adjacent right occipital lobe of the brain. The tumor measured 4.3 centimeters laterally and 5.7 centimeters vertically and 4 centimeters in an anterior-posterior direction. The medical examiner with these findings of the autopsy suggested to the Safety Board investigating the disaster that the tumor "could have affected the captain's vision, particularly where peripheral vision was concerned."

But the Board did not agree. If found that the tumor did not contribute to the accident, and the hypothesis that the captain might not have detected movements in the altimeter and vertical speed indicators was discounted. The fact also that the engineer's medical certificate revealed that "he shall possess correcting glasses for near vision" and he had tried to align optical sighting of the nosewheel had nothing to do with the crash cause.

The Safety Board blamed the crew for not monitoring the flight instruments more closely. No blame was attached to the light bulb. It was the Board's way of warning all flight crews that no matter how sophisticated or simple the instruments of the most modern of airliners, nothing can replace the human factor of eyeball vigilance at all times, particularly during the landing sequence, when most airplane disasters happen.

A truly glaring example of preoccupation in the cockpit, which safety experts fear is more common than uncommon, was revealed in the playback of the cockpit voice recorder from the ill-fated flight of Eastern Airlines' flight from Charleston, South Carolina, to Charlotte, North Carolina, on the morning of September 11, 1974.

Because of the fog that clung stubbornly to the slopes of the lovely Blue Ridge Mountains and filtered into the green-walled valleys of North Carolina that morning, the crew was directed by Air Traffic Control to proceed to the landing under "precise Instrument Flight Rules." There were broken clouds at 12,000 feet, a patch of open space, and more clouds at 4,000 feet. On the ground visibility was 1.5 miles and under no circumstances could the weather be considered hazardous.

At 7:32 A.M. the DC-9 crossed a radio intersection known as Ross. On time, the captain reported his height at 1,800 feet. He was at that moment 5.5 miles from the Charlotte Omni Range onto which he would "home" for his turn into the active runway.

But at nine seconds after this report the terrain-warning horn started its continuous tone. This meant that the airliner was at the 1,000-foot level or below. The landing gear was down and the crew was ready for the landing. Eastern regulations require the calling of altitudes by the pilot not flying the aircraft at hundred-foot intervals. This was not done.

Being advised by the captain that the flight was by the Ross intersection, the controller at Charlotte gave them the signal that they were cleared to land on Runway 36, the northwest concrete strip.

The reply from the captain was: "Yeah, we're ready; all we got to do is find the airport."

The first officer replied to the captain: "Yeah."

One half second later, both the captain and his co-pilot shouted. The aircraft struck a number of small trees, mushed into a cornfield beyond the trees, smashed into larger trees, and burst into flames.

Despite the proximity to the end of the runway the fire and rescue services of Charlotte Airport were unable to locate the crashed airliner and it was only through the efforts of a passing motorist and several residents of the area who had observed the final agony of the flight that the plane was found.

As is usual in all crashes, fire and rescue services are useless. Those who survived the crash were seated in the aft section and when it opened up like a split banana they were mercifully tossed outside. Even then it took forty-five minutes to start removing them to the hospital. While they were lying on the ground and suspended from small trees and bushes, fire consumed the wreckage and the occupants burned to death.

The scene was typical of most crashes. The forward entry door of the DC-9 was found to be open but had been jammed by a tree, and occupants were piled against this doorway. The forward galley door was blocked by a mound of earth. The auxiliary exit in the tail was not blocked but had never been activated for escape purposes. The center over-wing exits were blocked by fire. Only one small section of the airliner retained its structural integrity, said the Safety Board report, which says little for American engineering.

The occupant seat system failed, which is not unusual. This meant, according to the Board, that seat belts failed to hold the passengers and seats broke loose from their moorings, jamming together in a chain reaction and trapping the passengers in a steel-like vise. To this day, designers and manufacturers have not been able to solve a simple seat failure problem.

The Safety Board discovered from cockpit tapes that during the final descent the four crew members did not adhere to the landing sequence of the flight. The discussion among the captain and the others embraced such important subjects as used cars, politics, and other topics. During the last thirty-five seconds before the crash, they were discussing the location of an amusement park tower and this chatter was continuing while the DC-9 was below assigned altitude for the approach.

The Safety Board also learned that the crew paid no attention to the terrain-alert horn, which sounded loud and clear through the chatter of the amusement park tower. In the public hearing that followed the crash, it seemed apparent from the testimony of several witnesses that some pilots regard the terrain-warning signal as a nuisance and not a warning. That's because it sounds automatically on the final approach and if they think they are at the correct height the warning becomes a bore.

But in this case, the pilot or co-pilot, whoever was monitoring the flight, failed to call out the required airspeed and altitude, and the flight recorder disclosed that the approach speed was 168 knots when it should have been 122 knots for the DC-9.

The descent rate of the flight varied from 1,500 feet a minute to 300 feet a minute and then sharply increased to 800 feet a minute after passing the final approach fix beacon until seven eighths of a *second* before the impact. After the beginning of the terrain-warning horn this would mean the descent to the ground was in seconds and not in minutes as required by regulations.

The Safety Board was stunned. It was unable to determine the precise reason for the almost total lack of awareness during the final approach. It speculated that the crew relaxed its instrument scanning because of the intermittent visibility through the patchy fog sections and since they could see the ground from time to time they relied on visual clues rather than on prescribed Instrument Approach Rules.

In its conclusion to the report, the Safety Board repeated its earlier warnings, saying that the crash once again reflected serious lapses in expected professional conduct. Such a lapse in expected professionalism from senior pilots was never better exemplified than in the crash of the Pan American World Airways flight on a lonely tropical island earlier in that same year.

16

Death on a Tropical Island

It was raining in Pago Pago as the Clipper 707 began its descent for a routine refueling stop on its regular run from New Zealand to the United States.

Taking over the controls for the landing was Leroy Petersen, fifty-two, of Salt Lake City, a veteran senior pilot for Pan Am. Third Officer Richard Gaines would normally be seated at the engineer's panel but because the regular first officer had laryngitis and couldn't handle the radio communications, Gaines was filling in.

Captain Petersen had been off status from September 5, 1973, until January 15, 1974, for "medical reasons." Fifteen days before this flight Pan Am's medical department had qualified him at once for a return to flying duty. He had completed three takeoffs and landings on January 19 to requalify for the Boeing 707 in which he had been a pilot for fourteen years. Since requalifying he had flown 38.34 hours. He was a man with a long record of night flying.

Between the date of his release to duty and his return to the flight deck, Captain Petersen underwent voluntary simulator training covering heavy gross weight takeoffs, departure procedures, fire warning, fuel dumping, steep turns, stall, and particularly approaches using the Instrument Landing Approach System. The comment of his training captain was "Very good."

The total evaluation of his simulation training was attached to his record: "All work well done—good oral quiz—smooth pilot."

That flight of January 30 was operating on a routine run from Auckland, New Zealand, to Los Angeles with stops at Pago Pago and Honolulu. It was the kind of flight that all senior airline personnel bid for: long, uneventful trips uninterrupted by takeoffs and landings, no barrages of radio questions, no other aircraft traffic—nothing except the lazy absorption of sunshine and scenery over the entire route. Nighttime flying was just as delightful and there was a rest room on the plane for the crew if they got tired.

Three hours after takeoff from New Zealand the Clipper contacted Pago Pago Control and requested a weather briefing. At 2334.56 hours (Samoan Standard Time based on the twenty-four-hour clock, which would be approximately 11:34 P.M.) the flight reported it was at 5,000 feet and received the following signal: "Clipper eight zero six . . . roger . . . Pago weather . . . estimated ceiling one thousand six hundred broken, four thousand visibility, one zero [10 miles] light rain shower, temperature seven eight, wind three five zero degrees at one five [knots] and altimeter's two nine eight five."

Four minutes after this report, the crew received a second weather forecast because the rain showers were spotty and were just passing over the airport. Only seconds later the tower contacted the aircraft again but this time with an ominous message: "Clipper eight oh six—appears that we've had a power failure at the airport."

The co-pilot replied: "We're still getting your VOR [Variable Omni-Range radio beacon], the ILS [Instrument Landing Approach System], and the lights are showing, we got eight miles runway in sight."

If there was a blackout at Pago Airport it must have been in the Air Traffic Control area, which is located some 2,000 feet from the only runway and not visible from the landing strip. There is no control tower on the island because flights are infrequent.

"See any lights?" asked the controller. "We've just had a bad rain shower here and I can't see them from my position."

The co-pilot replied that the flight was five miles from the airport and the runway lights could be clearly seen, an indication at that distance that, if there was any rain, it was very light.

The runway at Pago was 9,000 feet in length and 150 feet in width, a narrow concrete strip hacked out of the jungle and connected to a small airport terminal. The controller told the flight there was no other traffic and to proceed to the runway and advise him when clear of the concrete.

"Eight zero six, wilco," answered the co-pilot. This ended the conversation with the center.

According to the read-out of the cockpit voice recorder, the captain asked the co-pilot if he could see the runway and the reply was that the lights were visible. This would indicate that Captain Petersen was flying the aircraft and his eyes were fixed on the glowing instrument panel. One might wonder at this point why he couldn't see the runway when the first officer said it was visible. All he had to do was lift his head and look although there is a possibility that his windshield was dirty, for at that moment he switched on the wipers and set the flaps at 50 degrees. This action completed the check list for the landing.

"You're a little high," the co-pilot remarked. Four seconds later a sound was recorded that could have been the trim actuator lifting the nose for the projected landing.

Five seconds later the radio altimeter warning tone sounded twice. The first officer interrupted the second warning with: "You're at minimums."

Two seconds later the first officer reported: "Field in sight."

Two or three seconds later the co-pilot, keeping his eyes on the speed of the jet and on the runway just ahead, reported: "Turn to your right—one hundred and forty knots."

These were the last words spoken in the cockpit. Seconds after this the 707 crashed into the jungle at an elevation of 113 feet and at the astonishing distance of 3,865 feet from the threshold of the runway. After striking trees, the airliner continued for 236 feet, smashing its way through thick jungle vegetation until it struck a 3-foot lava wall. The fire that started after the initial collision with the trees enveloped the aircraft in a mushroom of boiling flame. The death toll: 101 persons.

The four survivors who climbed out of the jet through the over-wing exits recalled there was little or no rain at the time of the accident. Fire was spreading rapidly and the screams of the trapped passengers could be heard above the roar of the flames. All those who died were the victims of smoke inhalation and massive first-, second-, and third-degree burns. The third officer survived the crash impact but died later from traumatic injuries and severe burns.

An investigation team of the Safety Board was quickly dispatched to the grim scene. It was immediately apparent that the crash was a survivable accident, meaning that the jungle had cushioned the force of the impact, and if fire had not followed the crash, the passengers and crew would have survived. The investigation therefore centered not only on Captain Petersen's performance and his ability to fly but also on survivability and the ability of remote airports to provide fire, rescue, and medical services.

Delving into Petersen's past, the Board learned that he had only once before made a landing at Pago, back in 1972. However, just before beginning his South Pacific runs on January 23, 1974, he had been shown a Pan Am training movie of Pago Pago Airport in order to familiarize him with the runway and the island terrain on the approaches. He had flown into Pago, according to his own flight log, on January 23, 1974, while en route to New Zealand, but investigation showed that the first officer performed the landing.

In order to repeat the behavior of the flight that night, the Safety Board was loaned another Pan Am 707 and a number of precision flights were made that followed the parameters of the flight recorder that was recovered from the metal skeleton in the jungle.

Over a period of weeks, duplicate descents and approaches were conducted, following Captain Petersen's precise altitude, the turns of the aircraft, and the speeds of the four engines. After passing across the line of restless surf, an incoming aircraft makes about a 3.5-mile approach over palm-studded land, including Lagotala Hill, which is located 1.7 nautical miles from the threshold of the runway. Lagotala has an elevation of 399 feet and from that hill the land slopes gently toward the airport. The entire area from the sea to the concrete ribbon is sparsely inhabited and is covered mostly with jungle.

If any pilot approaching Pago Pago were fated for trouble, Lagotala Hill would be the obvious source of difficulty. Therefore, pilots are specifically made aware of the hill during the familiarization training for flights into that island airport. Captain Petersen watched the Pan Am film, which shows how approaches are made over water with height being maintained until Lagotala has been passed over and then descent is made onto the only runway of the airport. He saw the hill in the movie and studied Pan Am's approach procedures over the terrain.

But what Petersen was watching on the movie screen was not accurate. The Safety Board had this to report: "Because of recent physical changes in the airport and a change in the reported elevation in Lagotala Hill, the portions of the movie which related to those items were outdated."

Whether the movie was correct or not, Petersen on his final approach safely flew over Lagotala Hill. The cockpit voice recorder revealed that his co-pilot reported he was 300 feet above the hilltop, which would mean his aircraft was approximately 700 feet above sea level at that point. His flight recorder confirmed this.

"Let me know when you have the runway," Captain Petersen asked his co-pilot just as he crossed over the hill. The reply was immediate: "Now you have the runway . . . you're a little high."

At this second Captain Petersen lowered the nose of the jet in a fairly steep approach glide. As he quickly reached an elevation of 400 feet above the ground, the co-pilot, who was supposed to call out the minimums in this flight according to regulations, did not do so. He did say, however, that the speed was 150 knots. Seconds later he told the captain that the aircraft was at minimums in height and the field was in sight about a mile ahead.

Captain Petersen made no mention that he ever saw the airport.

The co-pilot advised him to turn to the right, and Petersen turned, leveled out slightly at 140 knots, and then lowered the nose again. But he was only at 200 feet and almost a mile from the airport.

The cockpit recorder reported the final drama. Seconds after this last conversation there was a sound of violent impact.

On November 8, 1974, the Board determined that the probable cause of the crash was the failure of the pilot to correct an excessive rate of descent. The Board was critical of the entire landing operation for its severe lack of professionalism.

"The flight crew did not monitor adequately the flight instruments after they had transitioned to the visual portion of the Instrument Landing Approach . . . did not detect the increased rate of descent . . . lack of co-ordination resulted in inadequate altitude callouts . . . inadequate instrument cross-checks by the pilot not flying the aircraft and inadequate procedural monitoring by other flight crew members."

In their lengthy conclusion in this investigation the Safety Board made the following findings:

1. The captain had been off flying status for 132 days before the start of Flight 806.
2. There was no evidence of pre-impact structural failure, fire, or flight control or powerplant malfunction.
3. All components of the ILS to Runway 5 were operated properly.
4. The crew was not specifically told that the visibility was rapidly decreasing at the airport although the fact was alluded to by the controller.
5. The runway was in sight during the last two minutes and fifty seconds of the flight.
6. When the captain went "heads up," he apparently flew the aircraft using visual cues only and made no further reference to the instrument panel.
7. The required altitude awareness callouts and vertical rate of descent callouts were not made.

8. At no time before initial impact did the crew indicate any awareness that they were too low or that any aspects of the approach were out of the ordinary.

9. The approach environment may have caused the crew members to experience visual illusions and to perceive the aircraft's altitude to be higher than the actual altitude.

10. The captain's instrument scan proficiency probably was degraded because of his lengthy absence from flying.

11. The impact was survivable. Relatively minor crash forces were involved, occupant restraint was adequate, and the occupiable area of the aircraft was not compromised.

12. The injuries sustained by the fatally injured passengers as well as the surviving passengers were a direct result of the postcrash fire.

13. Only the co-pilot sustained traumatic injuries in the accident.

14. Only the left over-wing exits were used in evacuating the aircraft.

15. All surviving passengers reported that they listened to the pre-takeoff briefings and that they reviewed the passenger information pamphlets.

16. Fire and rescue response time was delayed by rain, barriers across the response route, terrain, and confusion as to what was burning.

17. Restrictions in the approach to the fire hampered fire-fighting effectiveness.

The Safety Board provided a shocking postscript to the story. It found there was only a one-lane road into the approach path of the airport and thus only one vehicle at a time could reach the fire.

"Had all the fire vehicles been able to approach the fire simultaneously, fire damage to the aircraft may not have been so extensive," said the Board.

The Safety Board was severely critical of the airport fire-fighting facilities. The fire crew at first thought that a house was burning and by the time they realized it was the downed airliner, it was too late to rescue anyone. The Board was also critical of the lack of medical services at the airport, but it could have examined almost any airport and found the same problem. It recommended to the FAA, however, that "minimum standards of medical services be established to ensure that mass casualties resulting from an aircraft accident can be adequately handled and satisfactorily treated."

The Safety Board pointed out that every airport serving United States flights cannot be certified unless the applicant can show a level of fire-fighting services and medical equipment appropriate for the various lengths of commercial aircraft.

But there was another element of danger on this flight, the Safety Board discovered, and that was the presence aboard the aircraft of hazardous cargo.

"The flight crew was unaware that hazardous cargo was placed aboard the aircraft," said the Board. In the cargo space was a quantity of ethyl methyl ketone peroxide, listed as hazardous because of its flashpoint. It had been placed aboard the flight in New Zealand and the flight dispatch papers did not identify the material. Neither the freight forwarder nor Pan Am was advised of the dangerous contents in the cartons.

The International Air Transport Association specifies that: "The maximum quantity of this material that can be packed in any one container is one half a kilogram (one pound) or one half liter (one pint). Plastic tubes packed with noncombustible cushioning and absorbent material which will not react to the contents and which will prevent breakage and leakage shall be packed in fibreboard containers up to a maximum of one half a liter."

This Pan Am cargo consisted of two hundred small bottles placed in plastic bags and then in tins, which were sealed. Four of these tins were placed in a fiberboard carton and the weight of the chemicals amounted to 4 kilograms, or 8 pounds.

Blatant disobedience of rules only comes to light after severe accidents. Passengers and crew, therefore, never know that a silent enemy may be accompanying them on their journey. Maybe it's just as well.

17

Deadly Poisons on Board

Trying to discover hazardous materials aboard airliners is an almost impossible task. In the United States there is a Restricted Articles Program within the FAA which enforces certain rules regarding packaging and shipping of restricted articles, but there is no program of surveillance of shippers' facilities that would detect the falsification of labeling. Spot checks by the FAA on suspected lots turn up hundreds of cases of contraband cargo, and the more inspectors that are placed on the job, the more hazardous materials are found.

Recently, a leaking package on a domestic flight from Florida to New York was found to contain corrosive acid. The package was labeled "Machine Parts." Poisons and explosives are shipped in deliberately mislabeled packages in order to avoid examination and thus bypass the laws that forbid their shipment by air. (One package was marked "Sanitary Pads.") This shows the blatant contempt that many U.S. industries have for the safety of air passengers and crewmen. But this applies not only to U.S. shippers. The crash of the Pan Am 707 at Pago Pago turned up evidence of hazardous materials being shipped illegally—and had the aircraft not crashed they would not have been discovered.

There is no international law that forbids the air shipment of hazardous materials. Customs officials rarely open air freight packages, depending mostly upon waybills for identification, and all shippers must know this. The British government charged in April 1976 that the Irish Republican Army was receiving air shipments from the United States consisting of ammunition, dynamite, guns, powder, and warfare chemicals. Although the Secretary of State's department promised joint plans with England to solve the problem, the IRA is still receiving such air shipments.

There seems no way to stop the traffic except by periodic spot-checking in the United States. Other countries don't seem to give a damn. When an official of the Canadian Ministry of Transport was asked in April 1976 how many prosecutions had been made in Canada over the carriage of poisons and other hazardous materials by air, the answer was none.

Goaded by the Safety Board, the FAA made 9,053 spot-check inspections involving 58,000 man-hours in 1974, and found countless infringements of the law. Some 470 industries were deemed to be prosecutable. One giant in the film industry was fined $20,000. Pan Am, of all people, was fined $1,500 for failure to notify the pilot that dangerous cargo was on his flight, a freight service was fined $5,000, and an oil company, $7,500.

Hundreds of prosecutions were launched in 1975 and 1976 after more than 11,000 spot checks involving 66,000 man-hours turned up the presence of dangerous materials most of them on regular airline flights.

The FAA hopes to frighten American shippers into obeying the hazardous materials regulations. Foreign carriers continue to ignore the U.S. regulations since they come under the laws of their respective countries, and if poison gas or other chemicals were found on British airliners, for instance, the culprits would have to be charged and tried in England after formal complaints by the United States. No wonder the FAA throws up its hands.

At a recent meeting in Geneva between the signatory powers of the International Air Transport Association the problem of controlling and forbidding hazardous materials from aircraft was shelved. It could not be solved.

"There is danger to every passenger on all international flights," said Sam Langford, chief of the Hazardous Materials Staff of the FAA. "We cannot force foreign lines to identify the hazards and they are flown into our International Airports, creating a constant potential danger. I have yet to see one foreign package marked with identification of hazardous materials that is required by IATA Rules. Not one."

A classic example of subterfuge and contempt for safety regulations came to light after the crash of a Pan Am Clipper at Boston's Logan Airport on November 3, 1973. Unaware of the hazardous materials in the cargo hold, the crew was unable to identify the cause of the fire that erupted from the spillage of these materials and they died without knowing the awful cause.

Flight 160 was a scheduled cargo flight from Kennedy to Frankfurt, Germany, with an intermediate stop at Prestwick, Scotland, for cargo delivery and refueling.

Captain John J. Zammett, fifty-three, with First Officer Gene Ritter, thirty-four, at the co-pilot's position and Flight Engineer Davis Melvin, thirty-seven, at the engineer's panel, departed the runway at Kennedy at 8:25 with 52,912 pounds of cargo, of which 15,360 pounds were chemicals.

Thirty minutes after takeoff, as the Clipper moved through 31,000 feet to its assigned flight level of 33,000 feet, the crew smelled smoke. There is nothing more unnerving than the smell of smoke in an airliner and they had no idea at the moment where it was emanating from.

Because he was over Sherbrooke, Quebec, at the time, Captain Zammett called Montreal Air Traffic Control and received permission to turn around and head back for Kennedy. But minutes later the smoke had increased and he asked and got permission to descend to Boston.

An emergency was declared and all flights around Boston were diverted as controllers turned all their efforts to bringing down the jet safely. At 9:26 A.M., the Clipper had dived to an altitude of 2,000 feet over the ocean and notified Air Traffic Control that it was inbound for the landing. The Clipper asked for a radar measurement of its distance from the Logan runway because its own distance-measuring device had failed.

"You're forty to forty-five miles, sir, abeam of Pease Air Force Base," reported the arrival controller, giving also the order for a sharp turn into Runway 33-Left to save precious maneuvering time. The radar transponder faded from the ATC screen and the controller notified the flight to land in the blind, meaning that he should come straight on in and "eyeball" the landing without wasting the time of asking and getting permission for the coming sequences of landing.

A few seconds later a stunned group of tower controllers saw the Clipper dive into the ground 262 feet short of the runway. They could see smoke pouring out of the cockpit windows. There was a blinding flash and Clipper 160 blew up.

Debris was hurled into the air, giant pallets of cargo shot upward and outward and descended into the sea and into the ground in front of the runway. In thirty seconds an already alerted airport fire department poured thousands of gallons on the huge fire and exploding rubble in the cockpit area in the hope of rescuing the crew, but it was hopeless. The Boston Fire Department joined in a massive soaking of the unusually stubborn fire. Two fireboats hurled streams of seawater into the mass of flames to little avail.

All those fighting the fire did not realize it was chemically induced. When the Safety Board arrived on the scene, its investigators were curious about the heavy black soot on crumpled walls of the cargo compartments, and most particularly the thick accumulation on the grille around the hatch that led from the cargo area to the cockpit. They found severe pre-crash fire damage above and below the cargo floor and the ventilating ports had accumulations of soot around them.

It was determined that structural deformation had been caused by heat of over 1,000° F. Something very dangerous had been in the cargo of the Clipper—there was no doubt about that. The Safety Board launched an intensive investigation to try and determine the cargo contents and the shippers and a host of handlers in between. It was probably the most massive such undertaking in the history of the Board.

The detective story started in Scotland, of all places. Periodic orders for chemicals had started on September 24, 1973, from the National Semiconductor Corporation (NSC) office in Scotland to the Allied Chemical Corporation (ACC) of California and New Jersey. NSC advised Allied that the shipments of the orders were to be made by air. Allied then tried to work out an arrangement with a chemical firm to repack the items that were not of legal size for shipment. However, the firm contacted was not interested.

On October 25, purchase orders from NSC, Santa Clara, California, were sent to Morristown, New Jersey, from the Allied Chemical corporation's office in Los Angeles.

"Allied Chemical Corporation personnel were aware that the chemicals would be transported by air, but advised NSC that they would be packaged for surface transport," reported the Safety Board.

The articles destined for the East Coast portion of the huge chemical order were moved by P. Callahan, Inc., a trucker, to the facilities of the Seven Santini Brothers, a repacking and trucking facility in Maspeth, New York. The NSC traffic manager, according to the Safety Board, monitored the shipments and requested expediting trucking service because the materials were urgently needed. Since NSC did not produce such chemicals, they had no procedures or manuals for handling shipments of restricted articles.

The following items of restricted articles were approved for shipment:

Article	D.O.T. classification	Quantity per package	No. of boxes shipped
Butyl Acetate	(normal) Shipper classified as combustible liquid (IATA)		
Poisonous liquids N.O.S. (stripping solution A-20)	Poison B	55 gal.	1
Isopropanol	*Flammable liquid	10 gal.	10
Hydrogen Peroxide (containing more than 8% hydrogen peroxide)	Corrosive	1 gal.	16

*Classification depends on actual flashpoint.

Article	D.O.T. classification	Quantity per package	No. of boxes shipped
Xylene	*Flammable liquid	10 gal.	
Acetone	*Flammable liquid	10 gal.	4
Nitric Acid	Corrosive	5 pints	10
Methanol	*Flammable liquid	10 gal.	160
Hydrofluoric Acid	Corrosive	10 pints	3
			50
Sulfuric Acid	Corrosive	10 pints	
Acetic Acid, Glacial	Not Regulated	10 gal.	60
			9

Meanwhile, the MSC International Traffic and Manufacturing Support's traffic manager and purchasing agent made out the orders to have these restricted articles shipped on Clipper 160, and arrangements were then made with Interamerican Freight Forwarders, Lyon—Commercial and Export Packing Division, and the Seven Santini Brothers.

Interamerican is a cargo agent for the International Air Transport Association, the worldwide association of airlines that has been attempting to pass laws governing the carriage of dangerous materials. Interamerican had been appointed cargo agent for Pan Am and therefore as an agent of Pan Am, the vice-president of Interamerican signed the waybill based on instructions from NSC. According to the Safety Board, this vice-president had been given the list of chemicals from NSC over the telephone.

Chemicals from various places began to move according to plan to arrive at Pan Am's hangar at Kennedy Airport not later than midnight of November 2 in order to catch Clipper 160's flight.

On November 1, Santini furnished Interamerican with the specified number of packages and the weight of each chemical. Documentation for this shipment was sent via Burlington Northern Airfreight to Santini at noon on November 2.

In the meantime, the shipment of sulfuric acid had started on October 30, packed by Lyon—Commercial in Los Angeles. Three hundred pieces were readied for shipment, weighing

10,000 pounds. The bottles of sulfuric acid were packed in wooden containers with vermiculite as the absorbent material. None of the personnel interviewed by the Safety Board could remember seeing white CORROSIVE labels on these packages.

On October 31, TWA received two closed igloos from Burlington Northern Airfreight. According to TWA rules, the cargo rate agent should check the commodity against the IATA restricted articles regulations of the Air Transportation Tariff for its proper classification and labeling. However, TWA never opens restricted articles to check the packaging. And so on to New York they went without incident.

Back at the Santini Brothers in New York, the staff did not have the facilities to pour and rebottle chemicals, according to the Safety Board investigators. Santini had been an Air Industry Transport Board agent for fifteen years; yet investigation showed that no employee had been trained for handling hazardous materials. Santini did not affix the required THIS END UP labels. The FOR CARGO AIRCRAFT ONLY and CORROSIVE LIQUID labels required by IATA Regulations were also omitted.

At Pan Am's hangar, the loading people discovered that some of the tiers of packages had been stacked too high. They were instructed by the supervisors to lay them on their sides, including a pallet that was marked IBM. One of the loaders interviewed said that some of the packages were loaded upside down into the aircraft.

The Safety Board reported: "Although the FAA had authority to enforce certain rules regarding the packaging and shipper's certification of restricted articles, there was no program, either within the Department of Transportation or the FAA, which would provide surveillance of shipper's facilities or would detect improperly packaged, or certificated restricted articles before they are submitted for shipment."

The Safety Board was batting its head against a brick wall and all its members knew it. A year and a half before this Boston incident, the Board had recommended that the Secretary of Transportation establish a government-industry advisory group to study "the need for additional private or regulatory safety controls in air transportation of hazardous materials" and to "continue to pursue vigorously the stated objectives to develop a revised and standardized format for all hazardous materials regulations."

To the FAA, in June 1972, the Safety Board recommended a monitoring system of all air carriers as well as a training program on the handling of hazardous materials by the airliners, and a requirement that all airlines "have available one responsible, well-trained individual who is designate" to receive all hazardous materials shipments.

What prompted the Board to make this recommendation in June 1972 was a bizarre incident involving the shipment of radioactive materials.

"Bizarre" may be the understatement of the century. Some 917 air passengers and scores of airline employees were involved as the result of a shipment of molybdenum 99 on December 31, 1971, by the Union Carbide Corporation from New York to Houston, Texas.

Two one-pint plastic bottles were involved. Each bottle was encased in a lead-lined container and each container was placed in a wooden jacket that was, in turn, mounted into a shipping pallet.

A Delta Air Lines Convair 880 carried the radioactive shipment over a New Year's weekend. A leak was discovered after two whole days had elapsed. The airliner was grounded and decontaminated. But the aircraft had made eight additional flights after the leakage and the Atomic Energy Commission was hurriedly called in to assist in checking the ten cities involved in the flights.

Contamination checks were made on 124 passengers, their 271 pieces of baggage, and on 2 dogs, all on the original contaminated flight. Other passengers using the same plane were checked out by state health authorities. It was a tremendous task to track down all the travelers and others who might have come in contact with the hazardous material.

The Safety Board determined the cause to be "improper packaging" in a "poorly maintained reusable container." It found that a series of human errors helped to trigger the leakage—a plastic bottle top too loose, a gasket in unsatisfactory condition, the package left on its side during transport.

The Board estimated at that time there were no more than twenty people in the entire nation knowledgeable in the regulations governing the shipments of hazardous materials. But the recommendations by the Board following the radioactive incident, and investigations at the time of the crash at Logan Airport in Boston a year and a half later, disclosed that nothing had been done by the Department of Transportation or the FAA to enforce the rules and monitor the flights.

Someone had to die first. In this case, the crew of the cargo jet. They died in vain.

PART V

Air Safety Affects Everyone

18

Jets and the Environment

Since the beginning of commercial aviation, air safety has evolved around the catastrophic termination of a flight for one reason or another. But today it also has another meaning, safety of the air as well as safety in the air.

Therefore safety has a dual connotation and although there will be many who show little or no concern over the deterioration of flight safety, mainly because they don't fly, they cannot afford to ignore the hazards that modern jets and supersonics pose to the canopy of airspace which we call the atmosphere.

It would be impossible for anyone honestly concerned with air safety to ignore the impact that present and future jets will have upon our air, which is required to sustain all animal and vegetable life. For this reason, *Jet Roulette* briefly departs from the current catastrophic enigma of aviation accidents to the problem of atmospheric destruction.

This combination of hazards will undoubtedly cement the human forces for an all-out drive to make the air safe for flying and breathing. There may be nothing quite like fear to close the gap between fliers and non-fliers and the culprits are the current jets and the coming supersonics.

Like other fuel-burning devices, jet airliners pollute the atmosphere. A Boeing 707 on takeoff will deposit some 70 pounds of solids into the air. But all jets are offenders, as can be seen on any day while watching the landings and takeoffs from our airports.

As with cars, the more powerful the engines the more pollutants are released into the atmosphere, and because supersonics have the most powerful engines designed by science, they have become the number-one target of environmentalists.

The concern is not without foundation. Climatic uncertainties in the Northern Hemisphere have been linked to the pollution of the upper atmosphere, where only jets and supersonics travel. Since the industry stoutly defends the jets, a massive worldwide research program is now in progress to investigate the changing composition of the atmosphere and to determine the reasons for recurring weather changes within the seasons.

Already some scientists have forthright declared that jets have caused the changes in climate and that supersonics will damage the stratosphere to such an extent that life on earth will be endangered.

Governments are moving ponderously to limit the size of fuel-burning car engines, outlawing incinerators in favor of refuse compaction, and have placed time limits on belching chimneys for the introduction of water-washed cleansing systems. Some states in America have already taken steps to ban fluorocarbons that are emitted from canned cosmetics, and agricultural boards are studying the effects of nitrogen fertilizers because of their adverse effect on the atmosphere.

The jet and supersonic problems are much more difficult and perhaps impossible to solve as long as there are fuel-burning engines to power them. Other than environmentalists, no transportation groups or governments would seriously consider ending air transportation even in the face of dire reports from the scientific community.

But if the increased incidence of skin cancer continues and climatic changes threaten world starvation, jet service as we know it today will have to be curtailed and supersonic travel banned forever. Drastic measures? Yes. But already there are indications that any such action might be already be too late.

The coldest winters since the ice age have descended over

North America and northern Europe and Asia. Snow for the first time in recorded weather history has fallen over southern Florida, and islands of the Caribbean have experienced freezing temperatures. Snowfalls in the traditional snow belts of the north have risen from previous highs of six feet to more than a dozen feet in such places as northern New York State, Michigan, Wisconsin, the northwestern states, and all across Canada, a country referred to by the British as "Our Lady of the Snows."

Satellite observations are presently being conducted over Canada and the Arctic regions to determine whether or not the heat of the sun is being diminished by atmospheric pollution. The extent of the damage to the fragile ozone layer of the stratosphere that protects all animals and vegetation from the killing effects of the sun's rays is also being analyzed.

The United States Weather Bureau has already announced that air samples taken by high-altitude balloons support the charges that the ozone is being depleted. But scientists point out that ozone is an unstable gas and has always been subject to high and low volumes as it moves between the tropics and the Arctic in a never-ending cycle. Environmentalists charge that this natural balance has been destroyed by jet airliners.

Ozone is a delicate gas, pale blue in color, with a characteristic fresh odor, which floats on a sea of denser air from 55,000 feet above sea level to the upper limits of the atmosphere above 100,000 feet. In this cold inhospitable region of dark blue skies the temperature remains constant at 69.7 degrees below zero up to a height of 82,021 feet. There it begins to warm slightly to 40 below at 100,000 feet.

Ozone gas is formed by the action of solar ultraviolet radiation upon the thin supply of oxygen of the stratosphere, which is found from 30,000 feet to the edge of true space—the area in which jets ply the heavens.

When ozone collides with nitrogen gas that seeps into the stratosphere from natural or man-made sources, a number of compounds are formed, one of them being nitric acid.

Nitric acid effectively destroys ozone and nitric acid is a residue formed by the burning of fuel in jet engines. Because present-day jets fly no higher than 43,000 feet, which is the limit for their aerodynamic design, the nitric acid acid is often mixed with other gases of the atmosphere at this height to be washed away by thunderstorms or high-altitude wind systems. But supersonics deposit nitric acid in the most fragile region of the ozone layer, where the cleansing effect of storms is non-existent. Both are culprits. But supersonics are the most serious polluters.

Dr. Harold Johnston of the University of California at Berkeley, one of the world's leading authorities on atmospheric sciences, was the first to measure the effects of pollutants on the ozone layer. He calculated that a fleet of five hundred supersonics, flying an average of seven hours daily, would destroy half of the ozone in less than a year.

With half of the ozone destroyed, all the animals of the world would be blinded if forced to live outdoors. His associates went further. They said that all plant life would die.

Dr. Johnston's findings concerning the atmospheric impact of supersonics were presented privately to the White House because of the direness of his predictions, but someone leaked the forecast to the New York *Times*. The effect upon the scientific and environmental community was profound, to say the least.

When he appeared in Stockholm at a world conference of scientists, Dr. Johnston was challenged sharply on his views concerning the supersonic impact on the atmosphere, but he countered his attackers by saying that he had been studying man's impact on the atmosphere for more than a score of years and that the supersonics deposit ozone-destroying chemicals in the very area where they do the most harm.

Dr. Russell Train, chairman of the Council of Environmental Quality for the United States government, testified before the House that he agreed with Dr. Johnston's findings and that the destruction of even a fraction of the ozone would effectively decrease the shield that protects the earth from ultraviolet bombardment. He revealed that the depletion of this gas by a scant 1 per cent would increase radiation reaching the earth's surface eightfold.

Dr. Gordon MacDonald, a member of the same council reported that if ozone depletion continues at the present pace, all life on earth will effectively be wiped out.

Added to this gloomy picture are the charges that climatic changes are being caused by the shutting out of the sun's heat by an ice shield, which has been deposited in the atmosphere by conventional jets and will be reinforced by supersonics to such an extent that another ice age is imminent.

"The widespread use of supersonics would deposit 150,000 tons of water vapor a day into the stratosphere, which is above the level of effective wind circulation," states an information bulletin widely circulated in America by the Environmental Co-ordination Office of the government. "This causes a blanketing effect which will alter the temperature of the earth's atmosphere, a risk that man cannot afford to take."

"I am convinced that we'll have another ice age, certainly within the next five hundred years," said John Perry of the U. S. Committee for Global Atmosphere Research during a gathering of international scientists in Toronto in November 1975.

In Washington, Henry S. Reuss, congressional critic of the defunct supersonic program, charged that water vapor placed in the upper atmosphere would result in increased cloud formations that could significantly decrease the earth's temperature. He said that he possessed a secret industry report that predicted that regular supersonic operations would produce atmospheric changes that could alter the climate.

"Despite the study that predicted a destruction of part of the ozone," said Reuss, "the Department of Transportation informed Congress there was no scientific support for suggestions that supersonic transport would pollute the upper atmosphere."

The controversy rages on. Intense investigation of the ozone layer which will be completed in 1978 should settle the arguments. But already there is a sinister hint of trouble. The FAA admits it has received reports from airline passengers, as well as flight crews, who have experienced ozone "irritation" while flying at high altitudes, presumably at the 40,000-foot levels.

As a result of these repeated complaints of dry mouths, burning sensations, and dry throats, the FAA has decided on an advisory circular to all airlines and to scientific organizations asking for suggestions to protect the passengers from the ozone attacks.

An FAA spokesman said it takes fifteen to thirty minutes for a jet to pass through the fingers of ozone that unpredictably decend to lower altitudes.

"Higher concentrations of ozone at lower levels have been experienced particularly on some of the over-ocean runs and more particularly on the America to Japan routes," said one scientist associated with the FAA.

Asked if this phenomenon had ever happened before 1977, the scientist said no. But scientists have predicted over the past ten years that passengers flying at extreme heights in conventional jets and at standard cruising levels of supersonics would be bombarded by solar radiation and galactic cosmic rays.

All the predictions from the scientific world have not dimmed the enthusiasm of those who have experienced supersonic travel in the British-French Concorde. If the decision to go or not to go with the Concorde was left up to those who have flown it, the acceptance would be overwhelmingly in its favor.

"It was the most thrilling experience of my life," declared Eric Thorsen, an aviation buff and Toronto radio announcer who had purchased a ticket for the first flight two years before the inaugural. His one-way ticket cost him $750 and "was worth every penny."

People who have flown the Concorde believe that the attempts to stop its operations into the United States are political and supported by an aviation industry that is jealous of the British and French achievement. It so happens that the British and French governments also feel that the failure of American aviation to design a workable version of the supersonic created bitterness which eventually was directed against the Concorde.

They may be right. It is no mystery in the aviation industry that U.S. manufacturers were angered and embittered by the federal government's decision to abandon the supersonic program. President Jimmy Carter has said that the environmentalists won their battle against the American supersonic program. But actually the program was dropped because Boeing failed to design and produce a supersonic plane that could successfully cross the Atlantic if an engine failure occurred and the aircraft would be forced to fly subsonically.

(This situation developed in the Concorde in April 1977, when vibrations developed in one of the four engines of an Air France flight to New York City and the airliner was brought down to the subsonic zone, thus necessitating a landing at Halifax because of the enormous amounts of fuel that are consumed when such an aircraft flies out of its designed realm.)

So the Concorde's future looks bleak. It takes its due place in modern aviation history by its failure to live up to environmental and safety standards that people require.

It will, of course, be permitted by court action to fly into New York and, by individual invitations, into Miami, Houston, Chicago, Detroit, Buffalo, and Boston.

But eventually the environmental considerations will positively ban the Concorde from the sky and at the same time will probably force conventional jet airliners to lower cruising altitudes to protect the atmosphere as well as passengers and crews. This in turn will mean more planes in the crowded sky and make the safety goals suggested in this book even more difficult to attain.

Statistics may show that aviation is safe. But for practical purposes it is not safe enough. We have ample evidence of this from the events of the last few years. With a concentrated lobbying effort by the general public, flying may yet live up to its claim that it is the safest and most delightful way to travel.

Let's hope so.

19

In Quest of Safety

Airline catastrophes have accounted for 12,518 deaths during the last decade. In 1976 alone, 1,332 passengers died during scheduled air services around the world, a year that the industry spoke of as good. These figures do not include the number of crew members, non-revenue passengers, and children in arms because it is the policy of the safety-conscious industry not to mention them.

The whole matter of safety is treated in a ridiculously casual manner. Everyone who has flown is familiar with the flight attendants' instructions to passengers before takeoffs. The information they give is really inadequate if an emergency occurs, but the airlines don't wish to alarm the paying customers by issuing more detailed instructions. How much use are the following?

Fasten your seat belt. It is questionable whether seat belts have ever saved a life. They may have prevented injury from turbulence. But airliners should try to avoid turbulence in the first place, so seat belt usage is a protection against lawsuits. It has become increasingly evident that seat belts can actually contribute to deaths in fire-followed crashes. People who have escaped such nightmares have reported they had difficulty opening their seat belts and they saw others who were trapped in their seats by them.

Seats must be upright. During a violent stop or a severe crash, seats behave like accordions, breaking loose from their moorings, jamming forward, and trapping passengers. It doesn't matter whether the seats are upright or tilted back. A jammed seat and a fastened safety belt can create a one-way ticket to disaster. In an investigation by the British Air Ministry of a crash of an airliner into a row of Manchester houses, the only survivor was the only person aboard the crowded flight who was not wearing a seat belt. And the industry knows of this disaster.

No smoking. There is no record of smoking causing either fire, death, or injury in a crash. The hot engines and spilled fuel will do all that is necessary to cause an instant explosion.

Oxygen masks. The stewardesses tell you that if pressurization is lost, the masks will automatically drop and the passenger need do nothing more than place the mask over the mouth and nose, give it a little tug to start the mechanism working, and *voilà*, safety. In fact during a number of emergencies some oxygen masks have not dropped. But passengers are never instructed what to do in cases like this. They should be told to insert a dime into the oxygen mask slot, which will immediately release the mask. But then, that would be an admission that safety gadgets can go wrong—something that the industry doesn't want to admit.

And cabin depressurization is so rare that time spent on demonstrating how the masks will fall would be much better spent telling passengers what they should try to do in case of a crash, and particularly in the more likely event of a fire-followed crash.

Exit signs. A card which is supposed to be in the pocket at the back of every seat shows all the doors and window exits on a diagram. Passengers would be wise to note these escape routes when checking over the so-called safety features on the card. It would help if passengers were actually told what emergency exit to use, which window or which door and an alternate route if fire or damage prevents the use of any exits. They should be told how to open the door and windows. Most people falter when it comes to a rapid decision; they become unsure of what to do. Don't depend on stewardesses. They panic too.

Passengers should also be shown how to operate and inflate a descent chute. These often fall inside the door, instead of outside. Sometimes they fail to inflate. A one-minute lesson is not too much to ask to save a life. The same applies to life rafts.

Passengers are never told that the face, and particularly the mouth, should be protected in case of fire. Cushions and blankets, with which all airliners are adequately equipped, can serve as protection against smoke and flames. The attendants will never tell you this. You must know it yourself.

When to expect a crash? Any time during the landing sequence. Be ready for it. Don't panic. If you must wear a belt because of regulations, wear it loosely so that you can slip out easily. Know precisely the nearest escape routes. Memorize them. They're different in every plane. Doorways are the best exits, much better than windows, which are placed over fuel-filled wings. Look for doorways first and windows secondly. In case the emergency lights fail, which often happens, you'll be glad you memorized their locations. Never exit an airliner on the side where fire is visible. It's going to blow up on that side. Escape from the other side and take a pillow or blanket, as explosions are not pre-announced.

There are steps that the aircraft industry could take to improve safety. Within two years, airbags could be installed in airliners to cushion every passenger from impact in a crash. Within the same time period, new fuel tanks could be installed made of puncture-proof neoprene so that bulk kerosene would not spill out and cause fires. More difficult, but worthwhile, would be the installation of sprinkler systems in the passenger compartments and cargo spaces that would spew non-toxic fire retardants under high pressure to control the fire. Seats, rugs, staff uniforms, curtains, seat stuffings—all these items could be manufactured of fire-resistant materials. Most of them are not.

In the meantime, after installing these items as regular equipment on all airliners, science can continue in its quest for non-flammable fuels. The United States Air Force has been experimenting and actually using such fuels on a test basis for a number of years. Until solid or non-flammable fuels are ready for commercial aircraft, less explosive fuels now used by many airlines could be adopted by those that still use more dangerous fuels, actually at less cost to the users.

The United States has banned the use of JP-4 in domestic flights. But overseas flights still use this high-heat-producing fuel, which can be ignited by static electricity. Air Canada and Canadian Pacific Air Lines use it, as it has never been banned in Canada. It is banned for British Airways in England. However, most other countries use it. Why? It cuts down maintenance time of the engines because it burns cleaner.

The airlines know how many passengers are going to die. They have a formula that projects the death toll for so many million miles of scheduled operations. The industry was able to live with these cold statistics until the arrival of the Jumbos, which carry larger passenger loads. Crashes mean more loss of life now. So the airlines are faced with a dilemma. Either they must protect the passengers by every means at their disposal or be forced out of business by litigation settlements.

To sum it all up, air safety need not be a myth. But, as the facts stated in this book prove, the industry has been clearly foot-dragging when it comes to introducing safety improvements at the expense of weight and cost. It's time for the public to stand up and be counted. Write both government and industry officials, phone them, badger them with every means at your disposal. You don't have to fly to get involved. Your family's and your friends' lives may be at stake. And recent crashes have taken a toll of persons on the ground.

Indifference, lethargy, and lack of knowledge on the part of the public have contributed to the problem of inadequate flight safety. Now you have the opportunity to become part of the solution, and make "Happy landings" mean just that.